WORLD BANK STAFF OCCASIONAL PAPERS NUMBER SIXTEEN

This paper may not be quoted as representing the view
of the Bank and its affiliated organizations. They do not accept
responsibility for its accuracy or completeness.

WORLD BANK STAFF OCCASIONAL PAPERS NUMBER SIXTEEN

Edited by

Ian Bowen

Deepak Lal

Methods of
Project Analysis:
A Review

Distributed by The Johns Hopkins University Press
Baltimore and London

Foreword

I would like to explain *why* the World Bank Group does research work, and why it publishes it. We feel an obligation to look beyond the projects we help to finance toward the whole resource allocation of an economy, and the effectiveness of the use of those resources. Our major concern, in dealings with member countries, is that all scarce resources, including capital, skilled labor, enterprise and know-how, should be used to their best advantage. We want to see policies that encourage appropriate increases in the supply of savings, whether domestic or international. Finally, we are required by our Articles, as well as by inclination, to use objective economic criteria in all our judgments.

These are our preoccupations, and these, one way or another, are the subjects of most of our research work. Clearly, they are also the proper concern of anyone who is interested in promoting development, and so we seek to make our research papers widely available. In doing so, we have to take the risk of being misunderstood. Although these studies are published by the Bank, the views expressed and the methods explored should not necessarily be considered to represent the Bank's views or policies. Rather they are offered as a modest contribution to the great discussion on how to advance the economic development of the underdeveloped world.

ROBERT S. MCNAMARA
President
International Bank for
Reconstruction and Development

Table of Contents

vii

Glossary

ARI	Accounting rate of interest
BK	Bruno-Kruger
BT	Bacha-Taylor
IRR	Internal rate of return
LM	Little-Mirrlees
mrs	Marginal rate of indifferent substitution
mrt	Marginal rate of transformation
MSC	Marginal social cost
MSV	Marginal social value
NPV	Net present value
OECD	Organization for Economic Cooperation and Development
PRI	Poverty redressal index
QR	Quantitative restrictions
SER	Shadow exchange rate
SWR	Shadow wage rate
UHS	UNIDO-Harberger-Schydlowsky
UNIDO	United Nations Industrial Development Organization
VMP	Value of marginal product

Preface

World Bank project appraisors have been for some time among the most extensive practitioners of social or economic cost-benefit accounting. The vastly expanded attention of many economists in recent years to the conceptual foundations and the art of social cost-benefit accounting is, therefore, a welcome and challenging development to the Bank. It is hoped that the current debate over methodology will lead to a better understanding of what constitute socially beneficial projects and to a wider application of the advocated procedures.

Bela Balassa, David Henderson, Maurice Scott and Shlomo Reutlinger reviewed the first draft of this paper prepared in March 1972. The paper was also discussed at the series of IBRD seminars on Project Evaluation in October 1972 and comments made by members of this seminar were very useful. However, more than is usual, the disclaimers of their responsibility for the views expressed in the paper apply.

DEEPAK LAL

Introduction

The purpose of this paper is to compare and critically evaluate various alternative project selection procedures which have been put forward, particularly for application in less developed countries. It is meant primarily for operationally occupied economists who may be confused by the various brand names, as well as the esoteric and highly charged claims and counter claims made by the proponents of the different methods, and who, moreover, may want to learn how the different methods fit in with economic theory as well as their own immediate practical preoccupations.

Some Preliminary Theory

It is appropriate to begin by stating the obvious: cost-benefit analysis is undoubtedly the most used, and arguably the most useful, form of *applied welfare economics*. Its theoretical basis as well as its limitations are therefore necessarily those of its parent, *theoretical welfare economics*. This paper is not for those who deny any practical use for theory, but for those who whilst recognizing the limitations of theoretical welfare economics nevertheless feel that in our present state of knowledge it provides the only basis for making an economic assessment of investment plans and proposals.

The purpose of any project selection procedure must be to provide a decision rule for accepting or rejecting a project. The net present value *(NPV)* or the internal rate of return *(IRR)* of the project are the indices usually used. Our chief concern in this paper will be with first, what should be included in the time stream of benefits and costs; secondly, what are the relevant values of the various cost-benefit components; and thirdly, how the discount rate (or rates) needed for determining the *NPV*, or the cut-off *IRR* at which projects are accepted, should be chosen. Most of the differences in the alternative procedures relate to apparently differing prescriptions in these three respects.

It will be repeatedly emphasized in this paper that any substantive differences among the alternative procedures are in large part dependent upon differing assumptions about the relevant aspects of the economic environment in which the investment decisions are being made. One of the basic purposes of this paper will be to demonstrate that, *in principle,* most of the suggested procedures are equivalent, if the same assumptions are made about the economic environment, though naturally there are differences in *emphasis* as to which set of assumptions is more relevant for LDC's in general, and more importantly in the *practical* problems of estimating the relevant values to be included in the *NPV/IRR* index, with accuracy and ease.

The reason why *in principle* most of the methods are equivalent, given the same basic assumptions about the economic environment, is their common lineage—theoretical welfare economics. One of its basic results is that in a perfectly competitive economy (with no uncertainty about future tastes and technology), allocation of resources on the basis of market prices of goods and factors (for which markets exist) would result in Pareto optimality for a given income distribution.[1] Market prices of goods and factors would equate and equal the marginal social cost *(MSC)* of producing and the marginal social value *(MSV)* of using the relevant goods/factors. For a truly marginal investment project (in the sense that it does not alter the *MSV* and *MSC's* of the output it produces and inputs it uses as a result of its operation), the values of the output and inputs at market prices would provide the correct values to be used in determining the net present value of the project.[2] Market prices would be the "shadow" prices to be used in project selection.

If the investment project being considered is not marginal (or if there are externalities), and does affect the *MSV* and *MSC's* of its output and inputs, then the relevant measures of the social benefits and costs of the project will be the change in the consumers' and producers' surpluses caused by the

---

[1]Pareto optimality necessitates that for a given distribution of income:
  (i) the marginal rates of transformation in production of different commodities are equal to their marginal rates of substitution in consumption,
  (ii) the marginal rates of substitution between any pair of factors are the same in all the industries in which they are used,
  (iii) the marginal rates of substitution of any pair of commodities is the same for all individuals consuming both goods.
Given that the above conditions hold, a Pareto optimum will exist, such that for the given income distribution it will not be possible to make one person better off without making someone else worse off. Treating the same physical commodity at different dates as many different commodities, equivalent intertemporal marginal equivalences for an efficient intertemporal program can be derived. See Dorfman, Samuelson and Solow [8].

[2]The net benefits being discounted at the optimal discount rate which equates the marginal rate of transformation *(mrt)* in production of present into future consumption, to its marginal rate of indifferent substitution *(mrs)* in consumption, determined in a perfect market for intertemporal consumption.

project. This, in principle, will be the procedure recommended by *all* the project selection procedures we shall consider. In the case of the perfectly competitive model, valuation of the changes in producers' and consumers' surpluses, at market prices, will provide the correct indication of the net social benefits of the project.

To the extent, however, that the perfectly competitive paradigm does not hold—for example due to the existence of monopolies, taxes and subsidies, externalities, and/or increasing returns—market prices will no longer indicate the *social* costs and benefits of using and producing different commodities. The social cost to be included in the *NPV/IRR* index of social profitability, properly defined, will still be the marginal social cost of the various inputs used, and the social benefit will be the marginal social value of the output produced. However, the breakdown of the perfectly competitive assumptions results in market prices no longer equating and equaling the *MSC* and *MSV* of the relevant commodities. The market price will now equal either the *MSV* or *MSC*—and in some cases of rationing may not equal either. The problem then is to adjust the market price to obtain the relevant "shadow" prices, which are therefore generally needed in investment appraisal because of the divergence between the *MSC* and *MSV* of the relevant commodities.

If neutral fiscal devices (lump-sum taxes and subsidies) are feasible, then a full Pareto optimum could still be achieved if the government eliminates the divergence between *MSC* and *MSV* by suitably corrective tax-subsidy measures, thereby restoring the equivalence of *MSC* and *MSV* with the market price of the commodity. However, for obvious reasons it will not be possible, in most cases, to cure the divergence in this manner. In that case, the divergence between the *MSC* and *MSV* of the commodity may have to be taken as a datum (or a constraint) and the "shadow" prices corresponding to this constrained (or "second-best") welfare optimum will need to be computed. A large number, if not most, of the shadow prices which we shall consider are of this "second-best" kind.

Second, even if the government can eliminate the divergence between *MSC's* and *MSV's* by suitable tax-subsidy policy, it may take time for the divergence to disappear. Then current market prices will not equate the *MSC* and *MSV* of the relevant commodities, but it is expected that future market prices will. As investment takes time and its effects are extended into the future, it is clearly the *MSC's* and *MSV's* of the relevant inputs/outputs appropriately dated which will be relevant in working out the project's social profitability. If it appears likely that in the future an existing divergence between *MSC* and *MSV* will be corrected, the appropriately dated price which reflects the social cost/benefit of the project will not be the current market price, nor the current *MSC* and *MSV* of the commodity, but rather the "equilibrium" price which is expected to prevail in the future. In this sense, even when an economy is moving towards an optimal set of market prices, from a distorted current set, it may be necessary to use "shadow" prices corresponding to the *future* optimal market prices, rather than the *current* market or shadow prices for pricing inputs and outputs which form the time stream of benefits and costs of the investment project.

Third, even for a perfectly competitive economy, there will be different Pareto optima associated with different income-distributions. Judging between these different Pareto optima will necessarily involve normative judgments about the desirability of particular income distributions.[3] Even if agreement can be reached on the desired income-distribution, there will still be the problem of legislating this "optimal" distribution. Again if neutral fiscal devices in the form of lump-sum taxes and subsidies are feasible, the government would be able to achieve a Pareto optimum with the optimal distribution of income. If however, as is more likely, neutral fiscal instruments are not available, then the distributional effects of investment projects will also have to be computed, and judged against and along with their purely "production" or "efficiency" effects. These problems open up other areas where there may possibly be conflicting judgments, and hence prescriptions for project selection procedures.

Practical Problems

These theoretical problems are compounded by practical ones. First, even though there may be agreement about the nature of the correct prices to be used in project selection, there may, nevertheless be disagreement as to whether or not the existing divergences between MSV's and MSC's which effect these prices will continue into the future or whether they will change. Depending on what assumption is made about the future course of the economy, the "second-best" or "first-best" shadow price will be the relevant one to choose.[4] In a sense, this is an empirical question; but to the extent that future government policies are normally unknown, the element of judgment involved in deciding which of these alternative assumptions is relevant, when considering existing distortions in commodity and factor markets, will be of paramount importance in deciding which is the correct "shadow" price to use. Hence it is important to remember that differing prescriptions on alternative evaluation procedures will most often be due to differing implicit assumptions about the current and, more importantly, the future economic environment.

---

[3] It being noted that investment projects affect both the intratemporal as well as the intertemporal distribution of income; the former by the distribution of their net benefits amongst contemporaries at a point in time, and the latter by the distribution of net benefits as between generations, over a period of time.

[4] The second-best shadow price is that associated with continuing divergences, the first-best, that with no divergence, between MSV and MSC.

Second, though we have been discussing the evaluation of a particular project and the social valuation of its inputs and outputs in what may appear to be a partial equilibrium framework, in principle, any proper investment criteria must take account of the total (direct and indirect) or what are termed the general equilibrium effects of the investment project. Thus for instance if an industrial project employs some seemingly underemployed labor in the urban sector, the ultimate effects via the impact on rural-urban migration could be a significant change in total output of the economy. The shadow wage rate will then in this case have to incorporate both the direct and indirect (via migration) effects of increasing industrial employment.[5] The $MSC's$ and $MSV's$ which are taken as the "shadow" prices in determining the social profitability of the investment project, must therefore be the general equilibrium "shadow prices." This might appear to be an impossible task, but the relative merits of alternative investment appraisal procedures will depend upon their success in taking account of the general equilibrium effects of projects, which will in turn, if the procedures are to be *practical,* necessitate making certain simplifying assumptions about the economic environment. Once again, these assumptions, though empirical in nature, require judgment, and hence there can be disputes as to whether or not the simplifying assumptions are "realistic" or relevant or both. *

For all the above reasons, even though all the procedures we will consider start from the same theoretical foundations, and hence are identical if equivalent assumptions are made, they may nevertheless differ to the extent that, in practice, they emphasize one set of assumptions about the economic environment rather than another. Hence, the continuing charges and countercharges that a particular procedure has ignored or assumed away an important aspect of reality, and is hence invalid; as well as the impression conveyed to neutral observers of shadow boxing on the part of different protagonists, and bafflement at the conflicting claims and counterclaims that are made for different procedures. This, however, does not imply that in practice certain procedures are not more general and easier to apply than others. However, it may be more important to begin by realizing that the similarities amongst the procedures are far greater than the differences.

The Procedures

There are three main evaluation procedures (with different variants) which are really in the running for adoption by policy makers.[6] These are

[5] See Chapter II's section on *Labor* for a more detailed discussion.

[6] In Chapter I, it is shown that the Bruno-Kruger measure is really a variant of the shadow exchange rate methods, and hence there are really two procedures.

(a) the system suggested by UNIDO [32] (certain aspects of which are common to the procedures recommended by Harberger [11, 12, 13] and other writers on the subject [27]), (b) the procedure suggested in the OECD Manual by Little and Mirrlees [24], and (c) the procedures associated with names of Bruno [2] and Kruger [16].

As these procedures all relate to ways of adjusting or correcting market prices, the best way to compare them is in relation to the important distortions which exist in most economies and the adjustments they suggest should be made in arriving at the "shadow" prices which take account of these distortions.[7] The following sections of the paper will therefore deal in succession with (I) distortions in foreign trade, (II) distortions in factor markets, namely for labor and capital, (III) problems caused by a nonoptimal income distribution, which includes a discussion of the problem of "employment," (IV) the problems, if any, posed by inflows and outflows of foreign capital associated with particular investment projects, which includes the "debt servicing" problem, (V) the general problems of project evaluation in a second-best world, particularly one in which there are distortions caused by nonoptimal taxes and subsidies.

In the first four chapters of the paper we will adopt a piecemeal approach to the various distortions and problems, assuming that, apart from the specific distortion being considered, the economy corresponds in all other respects to the perfectly competitive paradigm. The last chapter will consider the problems posed as a result of the simultaneous existence of a number of distortions.

---

[7]The term *distortion* is used in its technical and convenient shorthand sense of any phenomenon which causes the equivalence of MSV-MSC-market price to break down. It should not be taken to have any necessarily normative significance in itself.

Methods of
Project Analysis:
A Review

I. Foreign Trade Distortions

One of the most important sources of divergence between the MSC's and MSV's of commodities in LDC's is the restriction of foreign trade by trade taxes and subsidies or quota restrictions or both. Trade distortions introduce two sets of divergences in the domestic price system: (a) between the relative prices within the traded goods sector and (b) between the relative price of traded to nontraded goods. To see this it is convenient to proceed in two steps. First by considering a simple numerical example in a model with only two traded goods, and then, extending this by including a nontraded good. Following this theoretical discussion, we consider how the alternative procedures deal with the two above sets of distortions, in practice. It should be noted that in sections below headed *Traded Goods* and *LM and SER Procedures in Practice* we assume that trade distortions are in the form of tariffs. This assumption is relaxed in the section headed *Quantitative Restrictions* where import quota restrictions are considered.

Traded Goods

Consider a perfectly competitive, open economy which produces two traded goods (say cloth and food) with two factors of production (capital[1] and labor). Under free trade and given constant terms of trade, the domestic

---

A fuller and more rigorous treatment of the issues treated in this chapter will be found in Lal [17].

[1]We assume away various capital-theoretic puzzles in defining *capital*. See Lal [21] for a discussion of these puzzles in relation to project analysis.

import/export prices of the two goods and rental/wage rates of the two factors will be the relevant "shadow" prices.[2]

Taking cloth as the importable, and food as the exportable, in this simple economy foreign exchange can be saved by producing more cloth and/or earned by producing more food.

Suppose, however, that instead of following the policy of free trade, the government imposes a tariff on cloth as it is a convenient way for raising tax revenue.[3] We are then asked to evaluate the relative desirability of expanding domestic production of the importable (cloth) and the exportable (food). To get the correct relative social ranking of these two industries it will be necessary to correct for the divergence in the *relative domestic prices of the two traded goods,* introduced by the tariff. The "shadow" relative price of the two goods is given by the relative *foreign* prices. The correction for the divergence can be done by either (a) taking the foreign currency prices of the two goods and multiplying them *both* by a shadow exchange rate *(SER)* (which on certain assumptions will be equal to the tariff on the importable), to get the "shadow" prices of the two goods in *domestic currency* which is the numeraire. This is the UNIDO [32]-Harberger [11]-Schydlowsky [27] *(UHS)*[4] procedure; or (b) using foreign currency as the

---

[2]In technical terms, in this model, the optimal pattern of production and trade will be uniquely determined by the tangency of the terms of trade line with the domestic production possibility frontier. The consumption point being determined by the tangency of the same terms of trade line with the highest attainable social indifference curve for the two commodities. As a result feasible welfare (given resource, technological and foreign trade constraints) will be maximized when the following marginal equivalence prevails:

$$frt = drt = mrs$$

where *frt* is the marginal foreign rate of transformation, *drt* is the marginal domestic rate of transformation, and *mrs* is the marginal rate of indifferent substitution in consumption of the two commodities. The relevant "shadow" prices of the two commodities are given by the international (frontier/border) prices of the two commodities. Furthermore from Samuelson's theorem on the correspondence of factor and commodity prices it follows that relative factor prices (of capital and labor) will be uniquely determined by the given international prices of the two commodities. If now even a single money price of a domestic good or factor is given, all other money prices, and the foreign exchange rate which converts foreign money prices into domestic money prices would be uniquely determined. Alternatively, if the foreign exchange rate were given, the domestic money prices would be uniquely determined. Moreover a change in the foreign exchange rate would have no real effects on the economy, as it would only affect the absolute level of domestic money prices, without affecting the relative price structure which would remain the same as that given by the unchanged international prices. The argument can be generalized to include traded intermediate goods and naturally carries over to the case of *n* commodities which are all traded. Furthermore the model can be made dynamic given the intertemporal vector of international prices of the commodities, which will uniquely determine the intertemporal configuration of production and trade; the associated "shadow" prices of the dated commodities and factors being determined by the terms of trade in each period.

[3]As a result we will now have a divergence in the marginal equivalences for optimality. Now $frt \neq drt = mrs$.

[4]*UHS*, hereafter, is used as an abbreviation for UNIDO-Harberger-Schydlowsky [ed.].

4

numeraire in which case the foreign currency prices of the two goods will be their "shadow" prices. This is the Little-Mirrlees [24] procedure.

To see this consider the following numerical example.

Numerical Example 1

Assume that the foreign price (c.i.f.) of cloth is $200, and of food (f.o.b.) is $100. The official foreign exchange rate is $1 = Rs 1. Also suppose that we observe the following costs of production of cloth and food:

1 unit of *cloth* requires 10 units of *labor* and 20 units of *capital*.

1 unit of *food* requires 15 units of *labor* and 2.5 units of *capital*.

The wage rate and rental rate, the same in both industries (as we are assuming no distortions in domestic factor markets), are Rs 5 and Rs 10 respectively. The tariff on imports of cloth is 25 percent. The domestic price of food is Rs 100. Thus,

Cloth — c.i.f. price, $200; tariff, 25 percent; domestic price, Rs 250.
Food — f.o.b. price, $100; domestic price, Rs 100.
Wage Rate—Rs 5; Rental Rate—Rs 10.

At the existing domestic market prices the domestic money costs of the two commodities will, in this case, be equal to the domestic money prices of the two commodities. There is no reason for preferring investment in the production of a little more of one of the two commodities rather than the other, as shown in the table below:[5]

Table I: Costs of Production and Prices

Good	Labor (units)	Wage (Rs)	Capital (units)	Rental (Rs)	Foreign Price ($)	Exchange Rate	Tariff (%)	Domestic Price (Rs)
Cloth (importable)	10	5	20	10	200	$1 = Rs. 1	25	250
Food (exportable)	15	5	2.5	10	100	$1 = Rs. 1	—	100
Laundry (nontraded)	6	5	2	10	—	—	—	50

However, the tariff has as it were introduced a wedge between the *MSC* of producing and the *MSV* of using a unit of foreign exchange. The *MSC* of "producing" foreign exchange will depend upon whether it is "produced" by an expansion of exports of food or by expanding import substitute production and hence a reduction in imports of cloth. If the increase in foreign

---

[5]Note that a third industry, laundry, is shown in this Table. This should be disregarded for the moment, but it will be introduced in the second numerical example.

5

exchange is the result of a combination of both export expansion and import reduction, the *MSC* of "producing" foreign exchange will be a suitably weighted average of the domestic resource costs of producing importables and exportables.

The *MSV* of foreign exchange is given by the value of a unit of foreign exchange to consumers. Just as foreign exchange can be "produced" by expanding exports and/or reducing imports, it can be "consumed" by increasing imports of cloth and/or reducing exports and consuming more of the exportable food.

We first show how on the various procedures, identical results will be obtained if a *single* conversion factor for converting foreign currency into domestic currency values is used. For simplicity, we assume that foreign exchange is "produced" solely by expanding exports of food, and "consumed" entirely by expanding imports of cloth. Then the *MSC* of foreign exchange is given by the domestic resource cost of a unit of food exports, i.e., (15×5) the labor cost $+ (2.5 \times 10)$ capital cost $=$ Rs 100.

The *MSV* of foreign exchange is given by the domestic price (value) of the units of imports of cloth, made possible by exporting one unit of food. As the foreign price of food is \$100, and of cloth \$200, one unit of food exported will enable 0.5 units of cloth imports. As the domestic price of cloth is Rs 250, the domestic value of the imports of cloth made possible by one unit of exports of food is Rs 125. Hence the *MSV* of the foreign exchange generated by exporting a unit of exports is Rs 125, while the *MSC* of earning the foreign exchange generated by a unit of exports is only Rs 100. Clearly the *MSV* of using foreign exchange is greater than the *MSC* of producing it. Evaluation of the social profitability of the exportable food at market prices will thus understate its true social profitability, as the domestic price of the exportable Rs 100 (which is also its *MSC*) is less than the *MSV* of the foreign exchange one unit of exports make possible, namely Rs 125. The correct shadow price of the output of food is therefore Rs 125 and not the market price of Rs 100. The shadow prices of the inputs will be the market prices. Hence we have the following social cost-benefit relationships of an investment project to produce one more unit of one or the other of the two commodities.

> *Food: Costs:* (15×5) labor costs $+ (2.5 \times 10)$ capital costs $=$ Rs 100.
> *Benefits:* $1 \times 125 =$ Rs 125.
> *Net Social Benefit:* $125 - 100 =$ Rs 25.
> *Cloth: Costs:* (10×5) labor costs $+ (20 \times 10)$ capital costs $=$ Rs 250.
> *Benefits:* $1 \times 250 =$ Rs 250.
> *Net Social Benefit:* $250 - 250 =$ Rs 0.

Thus investment in food is socially profitable, even though at market prices the private profitability in the food industry is also Rs 0. As a result at "shadow" prices production of food will be expanded. Thus we see that in this example with a tariff on the importable, cloth, the only correction we need to make to market prices is to the market price of a unit of the exportable to get its shadow price. This correction is to multiply the domestic price of food by $125/100 = (1 + .25)$. But remembering that the tariff on cloth is 25 percent, this shows that the domestic price of the other traded good, food, must also be multiplied by this tariff. Then 1.25 can be taken to be the *shadow exchange rate (SER)* by which the *foreign currency prices* of *both* importables and exportables must be multiplied to get the correct social investment decisions. The net result will be to make the relative shadow prices equal the relative *foreign* prices of the two goods.

Alternatively, if we used foreign currency as our numeraire, *and* converted the domestic money values of the factors of production into foreign currency equivalents *at the SER of 1.25,* then we could equivalently have determined the relative social profitability of the two goods as follows:

> *Food: Costs:* $(15 \times 5/1.25)$ labor costs $+ (2.5 \times 10/1.25)$
> capital costs $-$ \$80.
> *Benefits:* \$100.
> *Net Social Benefit:* \$100 $-$ \$80 $=$ \$20.
> *Cloth: Costs:* $(10 \times 5/1.25)$ labor costs $+ (20 \times 10/1.25)$
> capital costs $=$ \$200.
> *Benefits:* \$200.
> *Net Social Benefits:* \$200 $-$ \$200 $=$ 0.

(Note that the domestic factor prices have been converted into foreign exchange at the *SER* of $\$1 = $ Rs 1.25.) Clearly, again food production is socially more desirable, at the margin, than cloth production.

The latter procedure of working out the costs and benefits of the project in terms of foreign exchange would be the Little-Mirrlees *(LM)* procedure, *if we had used a single conversion factor equal to the SER to convert domestic money costs* of the factors of production into foreign currency.

However, as is emphasized in the next section, *LM do not generally use a single SER as a conversion factor for converting domestic money values into foreign currency,* and this leads to certain differences in practice when compared with the *SER* procedures. The former procedure using the *SER* of 1.25 to value the two traded good outputs is the *SER* procedure recommended by Harberger, Schydlowsky and UNIDO (the *UHS SER*). The two are equivalent in this case and merely involve a change in numeraire.

The third method, the Bruno-Kruger *(BK)* method, is also equivalent. By this method the domestic resource costs per unit of foreign exchange saved/

7

earned by the projects would be computed and the resulting ratios compared with the shadow exchange rate. This would yield for

$$Food: \frac{\text{Rs } (15 \times 5) + (2.5 \times 10)}{\$100} = 1 < 1.25$$

(the shadow exchange rate assumed is $\$1 = \text{Rs } 1.25$)

$$Cloth: \frac{\text{Rs } (10 \times 5) + (20 \times 10)}{\$200} = 1.25$$

and clearly again an increase in food production should be favored as compared with an increase in cloth production.

Next, we relax our simplifying assumption that foreign exchange is "produced" solely by increasing exports of food, and "consumed" only by increasing imports of cloth. We first consider the case with *domestic currency as the numeraire*.

The *MSC* of producing foreign exchange by expanding food or cloth production are still given in this more general case by the domestic costs of producing the two goods. What of the *MSV* of "consuming" foreign exchange. A unit expansion of the cloth (food) industry results in foreign exchange earned of $200 ($100). Now suppose that a unit increase in foreign exchange is "consumed" by increasing imports of cloth of α, and decreasing exports of food of β, in foreign exchange (with $\alpha + \beta = 1$). The *MSV* of a unit of foreign exchange will then be the domestic value of $\$\alpha$ of imports of cloth plus $\$\beta$ of exports of food. This is given by: $[(\alpha/200) \times 200 \times 1.25 + (\beta/100) \times 100 \times 1] = [(\alpha \times 1.25) + \beta]$. Let us denote this by E, and it will be the *SER* in this more general case. We can now determine the relative social profitability of the two goods, which will be:

Food: *Costs:* Rs 100 (as before).
        Benefits: $\$100 \times E = \text{Rs } 100E$.
        Net Social Benefits: Rs $100E$ − Rs 100 = positive.
Cloth: *Costs:* Rs 250 (as before).
        Benefits: $\$200 \times E = \text{Rs } 200E$.
        Net Social Benefits: Rs $200E$ − Rs 250 = negative,

as the value of E must lie between $\$1 = \text{Rs}$ (when $\alpha = 0$) and $\$1 = \text{Rs } 1.25$ (when $\beta = 0$). Hence as before food production will be socially more profitable than cloth.

Alternatively, we could have taken *foreign currency as the numeraire*. The social profitability of food and cloth production would be determined as follows. The *MSV* of the two goods would still be given by their foreign exchange prices. What of the *MSC's?* These will consist of the foreign exchange equivalent values of the primary factors used in the production of the two goods. We could convert the domestic money values of these primary factors into foreign exchange values at the general *SER* of E, and we would

8

then obtain an identical result as in the case with domestic currency as the numeraire.[6] However, in general, the use of a *single* conversion factor for converting the factor prices into foreign exchange equivalents will not be correct. For the factor prices to be used in our social profitability calculations should be the opportunity costs of these factors in terms of foreign exchange in an alternative use. This opportunity cost will be equal to the foreign exchange value marginal product *(VMP)* of the factors in the industries from which they are drawn for use in the industry whose output is being expanded. Thus the foreign exchange *VMP* of labor (capital) in an alternative use when the food industry is being expanded is the foreign exchange *VMP* of labor (capital) in cloth production (given our implicit full employment assumption); and conversely for expansion of the cloth industry. Thus the shadow price of labor for the food industry is $5/1.25 = 4, and for the cloth industry is $5/1 = 5; while that for capital is $10/1.25 = 8 for the food industry, and $10/1 = 10 for the cloth industry; where the conversion of domestic *VMP* into foreign exchange *VMP* of factors *from* the food (cloth) industry is done at the effective exchange rate which applies to food (cloth) output, namely $1 = Rs 1 (1 = Rs 1.25)$.[7] The relative social profitability of the two goods is then,

> *Food: Costs:* (15×4) labor $+ (2.5 \times 8) = 80.
> *Benefits:* $100 (as before).
> *Net Social Benefits:* $20.
> *Cloth: Costs:* (10×5) labor $+ (20 \times 10)$ capital $= 250.
> *Benefits:* $200 (as before).
> *Net Social Benefits:* $- 50,

and once again food is more profitable than cloth. *This is the general LM method,* and it will rank the projects in the same order as the *SER* method. However, note that whereas the *SER* method averages across the implicit effective exchange rates on food and cloth (by applying the weights α and β), the *LM* method actually uses the multiple effective exchange rates as conversion factors. As such it is likely to be more accurate, as well as easier to apply, as it is not easy to decide what weights α and β should be used in determining the average *SER* on the alternative methods.

Finally, the third method *BK* will once again be a straightforward transformation of the *SER* test. In the inequalities we have derived above for this method, in this more general case we will now have to substitute E for 1.25 as the *SER* on the right-hand side.

---

[6] This was the assumption we made in the first case above, but as we emphasized this is *not* the general practice recommended by *LM*.

[7] Thus, the correct relative social profitability on *LM* lines of the two industries in example 1 of the first case would also be given by the calculations which follow.

Thus on all three procedures in this simple model with only traded goods, the major adjustment which is required to get the right social investment decisions is to correct for the *divergence between the relative prices of the two traded goods,* caused by the protective structure, and all three procedures will give identical social rankings of the two industries.

Nontraded Goods

The above case is however extremely simplified, as it did not include nontraded goods. The introduction of these goods introduces *another* distortion resulting from the protective structure. In addition to the distortion of the relative prices *within the traded goods sector* (which was the only distortion in the previous case) there will now be a further distortion *in the relative prices of traded to nontraded goods* resulting from protection. The adjustments which are necessary to obtain the correct social investment decisions will moreover depend upon whether the existing protective structure is assumed to (a) remain unchanged, or (b) to be removed, in the future. If it is assumed to remain unchanged, then the only adjustments required are those for the distortion in relative prices of traded goods, discussed in the previous section. If however, the economy is assumed to move to free trade, then it will be necessary to estimate (i) the relative fall in the price of the traded and nontraded goods, which can occur via an exchange rate change (assuming a fixed domestic money price of the nontraded good) or a fall in the price of the nontraded good (assuming a fixed exchange rate)[8] (ii) the change in the wage-rental ratio which will accompany the change in the relative price of traded to nontraded goods. Given estimates of these changes, the two basic alternative procedures—(1) the *SER* method which uses domestic currency as the numeraire, and (2) the *LM* method which uses foreign currency as the numeraire—will give identical social rankings of the two industries. The *SER* to be used as procedure (1) will, however, not be the *MSV* of foreign exchange in the protection situation as in the previous section (the *UHS SER*), but will be the "equilibrium" free trade exchange rate. (This can be called the Bacha-Taylor *(BT) SER,* after the joint authors who have recommended its use [1].)

To see this consider the following numerical example.

Numerical Example 2

We expand our previous numerical example by including a third, nontraded, good called Laundry, the domestic price of which is Rs 50 per unit. The costs of production of Laundry in the protection situation are:

---

[8]Or a combination of the two.

One unit of *laundry* requires 6 units of *labor* and 2 units of *capital* and as the wage rate is still assumed to be Rs 5, and the rental rate of capital, Rs 10, the domestic money costs of production of laundry are Rs 50, which is also its domestic money price. Hence as in the case of food and cloth (the two traded goods) there will be no reason for preferring investment in the production of a little more of one of the three commodities rather than the other two. However for the reasons noted in the case with only two traded commodities, valuation at domestic market prices understates the relative social benefit from producing food rather than cloth, and adjustments on the lines of any of the three evaluation procedures will correct for this in an equivalent manner. But what of comparisons of investments in laundry production with either food or clothing? This will depend crucially upon whether or not the existing protection structure will be maintained.

First assume that the *existing protection structure is expected to remain unchanged.* As *ex hypothesi,* a marginal investment project will not change the wage-rental rates, the *MSC's* of production of the three commodities, taking *domestic currency as the numeraire* are still given by their market costs of production. It is still however necessary to make corrections to the values of the three goods, to obtain their *MSV's.* In domestic currency the *MSV* of cloth is Rs $(200 \times E) =$ Rs $200E$, the *MSV* of food is Rs $(100 \times E) =$ Rs $100E$ (for the same reasons as in the pure traded goods case), and that of laundry is Rs 50. (The market prices are Rs 250, Rs 100 and Rs 50, respectively; see Table I.) Hence in this case, like the case with only traded goods, the only adjustment is the correction for the distortion between the *MSC* and *MSV* of producing and using a unit of foreign exchange, which is done by using a *SER* of E (whose value lies between 1.25 and 1) to convert the foreign prices of both food and cloth into their *MSV's* in *domestic currency.* This is the practice recommended by *UHS.*

Alternatively we could have used *foreign currency* as the numeraire following the *LM* method. The *MSV's* of the two tradeable goods food and cloth would still be their foreign exchange "border" prices, and if the factors employed in their expansion are drawn from the other tradeable good industry, the foreign exchange *VMP* of the factors in the traded good industry from which they are drawn would be the "shadow" factor prices, and the *MSC* of production of the two traded goods would be determined as in the first numerical example's second case. What if the factors are drawn from the nontraded good industry, laundry; and what will be the shadow price of the output of laundry?

The answer to the last part of the question is that if (as *LM* assume) the demand and supply for nontraded goods is always kept in balance (and as we should make explicit, nontraded goods are produced under constant cost

11

conditions) the *MSV* of the nontraded good will equal its *MSC*. The latter can be determined directly from the cost conditions of laundry production, with the primary factors being valued at the foreign exchange *VMP* in the traded good industry (food or cloth or both) from which they are drawn. Note that as the *MSV* = *MSC* for laundry, the net social benefits of laundry production will be zero.[9]

This leaves the question of determining the shadow prices of primary factors drawn from the production of laundry (the nontraded good) to expand the output of cloth (food). The first round effect of this will be to reduce the output of laundry (as we are assuming full employment of the factors), which will tend to raise its domestic money price (as by definition all domestic demand for nontraded goods is met from domestic production), and hence raise the domestic money wage and rental rates in the laundry industry (as these are equal to the now higher *VMP* in domestic currency of the two factors in laundry production). This in turn will induce factors from the third industry food (cloth) to flow into laundry production (as the *VMP's* and hence factor prices in domestic currency in food [cloth] are unchanged given the fixed border price of food [cloth]). This will reduce the wage-rental rates in laundry production, and hence the price of laundry in the second round back to their original values (assuming that all changes are *marginal* displacements around an equilibrium position). The net effect of expanding cloth (food) production will have been to reduce *indirectly* the output of food (cloth), with the factors required for expanding cloth (food) output coming *indirectly* from the food (cloth) industry, even though the first round effect is on the nontraded good industry, laundry.

Hence, the shadow prices of the factors in cloth (food) industry will still be their foreign exchange *VMP's* in the food (cloth) industry, that is, $4 ($5) for labor, and $8 ($10) for capital. The rankings of the three industries is then given by their relative net social benefits which are

    Food: $20 (from the second case in numerical example 1)

    Laundry: 0 (from above)

    Cloth: $50 (from the second case in numerical example 1)

It should however be noted that, in general, when resources are withdrawn from the nontraded good industry (laundry), output and hence *consumption* of laundry *could* fall, and hence the implicit assumption made above, that the final effect is entirely on the output of traded goods, would be invalid.

---

[9]Thus, if laundry expansion draws upon primary factors *from,* say, the food industry, the *MSC* of a unit of laundry production *and* the value of a unit of its output, in foreign exchange, will be: (6 × $5) labor + (2 × $8) capital = $40. As the social costs *and* benefits are both $40, the *net* social benefit is 0. Alternatively, if laundry expansion draws primary factors from the cloth industry, the social costs and benefits are (6 × $5) labor + (2 × $10) capital = $50, and once again, as *ex hypothesi MSC* = *MSV* of nontraded goods, the net social benefit is 0.

The foreign exchange equivalent value of any such consumption foregone, would be obtained by using a *consumption conversion factor* which is normally derived on the *LM* method in the estimation of their shadow wage rate. This converts the value of Rs 100 of domestic consumption in domestic currency into say y of foreign currency equivalent. This is done by revaluing the goods (and services) which enter into consumption at domestic prices (obtained from consumer expenditure surveys) into their "border" price equivalents. This consumption conversion factor is the closest analogue to the estimation of an *SER* on the *LM* method. But note that if it is possible to identify the groups whose consumption is affected and their pattern of expenditure is known, then on *LM* lines there will be a multiplicity of consumption conversion factors estimated.[10] Once such a conversion factor (or factors) has been derived, the conversion of say Rs n of consumption foregone of laundry, in domestic currency, can be converted into the foreign exchange equivalent value, by using the conversion factor of $y = $ Rs 100 to obtain the *MSV* of the foregone consumption in foreign exchange as $y·n/100$.

Thus both the *LM* and *SER* methods (as well as the *BK* ratio which will just be a straightforward transformation of the *SER* test) will give the identical ranking of industries. However, as before, unlike the *SER* method, which averages across the effective multiple exchange rates on the traded commodities, the *LM* method in deriving its shadow prices will use explicit multiple conversion factors which correspond to the extant multiple exchange rates.

Second, assume that *the protective structure will be removed in the future.* Clearly the relevant shadow prices for evaluating the desirability of investment in food, clothing and laundry will now be the *MSC's* and *MSV's* of the goods and factors in the free trade situation. With the removal of the tariff of 25 percent on imports of cloth, the relative domestic prices of the three goods (at the protection exchange rate of $1 = $ Rs 1) will change. With a reduction in the price of cloth relative to both the prices of food and laundry, there will be a shift in domestic consumption from food and laundry towards cloth (assuming unrealistically that cloth, laundry and food are close substitutes), and of domestic productive resources from production of cloth to production of food and laundry. Now consider the markets for food, cloth and laundry. In the market for cloth there will be excess demand, while in the markets for food and laundry there will be excess supply. Moreover unless the excess demand for cloth is matched by an equivalent excess

---

[10]For estimates of a conversion factor for the consumption of agricultural households in Maharastra see Lal [21], while Scott, MacArthur and Newberry, *Project Appraisal in Practice* (forthcoming) and Lal, *Men or Machines* (forthcoming) have estimates for the multiple conversion factors for Kenya and the Philippines respectively.

supply of food (an exceptional circumstance), there will tend to be a balance of payments deficit, given by the differences between the excess demand for cloth and the excess supply of food. What is more, from Walras' Law, this net excess demand for the two traded goods must be exactly equal to the excess supply of the nontraded good, laundry. In the next stage therefore to restore equilibrium, it will be necessary to cure the balance of payments deficit, that is to eliminate the net excess demand for tradeables which is equivalent to eliminating the excess supply for the nontraded good. *This requires a fall in the relative price of the nontraded to the traded goods.*

The above change can be brought about by two alternative mechanisms (or a combination of both). The first with the *exchange rate fixed, and the domestic money price of the nontraded good, laundry, flexible.* The second, is with the *domestic money price of the nontraded good fixed and a flexible exchange rate.* As the same relative price of traded to nontraded goods needs to be established (on either adjustment mechanism) to restore equilibrium, the necessary fall in the price of the nontraded good (with a fixed exchange rate) must be equal to the required devaluation of the exchange rate (with the price of the nontraded good fixed). As a result the domestic money prices of the three goods will be the same in free trade on both adjustment mechanisms. Hence they will lead to identical resource allocation effects and factor price changes from the protection situation.

Assuming that we know or can guess the changes in the wage and rental rates and the exchange rate or the price of the nontraded good from the protection to the free trade situation, then either of the two alternative methods of using domestic currency as the numeraire and a *SER,* or foreign currency as the numeraire and the *LM* procedures, will give identical rankings of the relative social profitability of investment in the three industries. Note however that the relevant *SER* will not be the *SER* which was derived for the case when existing protection is assumed to continue, but will be the "equilibrium" free trade exchange rate (the *BT SER*).

Alternative Procedures

We are now in a position to compare the alternative procedures which have been suggested to take account of trade distortions in developing countries. *First,* there are the *SER* methods. There are two subdivisions within these depending upon the particular assumptions made about future trade liberalization.

(1) The UNIDO [32]-Harberger [11]-Schydlowsky [27] *(UHS) SER* method. This obtains the *SER* as the *MSV* of foreign exchange in the *protection* situation, as the "weighted sum of domestic prices of traded goods, divided by a similar weighted sum of world prices, the weights in each case

being the marginal changes in imports and exports induced by the project."[11] The *UHS SER* is then used to shadow price all the traded inputs and outputs by converting their foreign currency values into domestic money shadow prices at the *SER*. If the only distortions are those caused by foreign trade taxes and subsidies,[12] the shadow prices of the remaining nontraded goods and the factor prices would be the market prices in the protection situation. This method is clearly valid, on the assumption that the *existing protection structure will remain unchanged.*

(2) The "equilibrium" *SER* method, most recently advocated by Bacha and Taylor *(BT)* [1]. This method first works out the "equilibrium *SER*," which would exist after trade liberalization, in free trade.[13] The foreign currency values of traded goods are next converted into shadow prices by multiplying them with this *BT SER,* while the prices of nontraded goods are taken as the market prices in the protection situation. This procedure is clearly valid if it is assumed that *trade-liberalization will take place with exchange*

---

[11]The formula for calculating the *UHS SER* is: (see [32], p. 2.5 and following)

$$UHS\ SER = \sum_{i=1}^{n} f_i \frac{P_i^D}{P_i\text{c.i.f.}} + \sum_{i=n+1}^{n+h} x_i \frac{P_i^D}{P_i\text{f.o.b.}}$$

where f_i — is "the fraction of foreign exchange allocated to imports of the ith of n commodities at the margin."

x_i — is the "rupee amount by which each of h exports falls in response to earnings of foreign exchange."

P_i^D — are the domestic market clearing prices of imports and exports, that is inclusive of trade taxes (and subsidies).

$P_i\text{c.i.f.}$ and $P_i\text{f.o.b.}$ are the "border" prices of imports and exports. Maurice Scott in his written comments has pointed out that this formula "assumes that relative *domestic* prices of traded goods correctly measure their relative marginal contributions to aggregate consumption. This *could* be right, but it certainly *need* not, especially if the traded goods in question are intermediate products subject to varying tariffs or quotas or both. It therefore seems to me that the formula is conceptually wrong as well as being operationally difficult to apply." The correct *SER* for UNIDO, he feels, "is the ratio of the domestic to the foreign exchange cost of a marginal increase in aggregate consumption. In *LM* terms this would be the conversion factor for marginal consumption expenditures."

[12]But see the qualifications in the previous footnote.

[13]The formula for calculating the *BT SER* is: (see[1])

$$BT\ SER = r \left[\sum_j \Phi_j \left(V_j E_j^x \right) \sum_i \gamma i \left(- \Psi_i N_i^m \right) \right] \Big/ B$$

where r — is the protection exchange rate.

Φ_j — is the "force of the export, tax or subsidy" on j^{th} export.

γi — is the "force of the tariff" on i^{th} good.

$V_j\ (\Psi_i)$ — are the shares of exports (imports) of sector $j(i)$ in total exports (imports).

E_j^x — is the price elasticity of export supply of the jth good.

N_i^m — is the price elasticity of import demand of the ith good.

and $B = \sum_j V_j E_j^x - \sum_i \Psi_i N_i^m$

15

rate flexibility and the prices of nontraded goods inflexible. However as trade liberalization and the exchange rate change (in the movement, to free trade) will have altered the relative prices of all commodities (see Table II) it will also lead to a change in relative factor prices in the free trade as compared with the protection situation. Thus, for the procedure to result in correct investment decisions, in addition to shadow pricing traded goods by using the *BT SER (e*)*, it is also necessary to determine the *factor prices in free trade (W*, R*)*, and use these to value the primary factors used in the project.

Second, there is the *Bruno-Kruger (BK) ratio* [2], [16]. As can be seen from the first numerical example given above, the *BK* ratio is derived by a mere rearrangement of the terms used in deriving the rates of return on the *SER* methods. Given the same assumptions about trade liberalization, it will give the same ranking of industries as the *UHS SER* (if there is no trade liberalization) and the *BT SER* (if there is trade liberalization). The cut-off exchange rates with which the *BK* ratio is compared being the *UHS SER* in the first case and the *BT SER* in the second. Primary factors being priced at market prices in the protection situation in the first case, and at the free trade factor prices in the second. As the method requires the same information as the *SER* methods, and is really just a variation of these methods, it can be subsumed under them. However, the resulting ratio does not have obvious intuitive links to capital and growth theory in contrast with rate of return measures, and this could be a disadvantage. Also, in the past most investment appraisal has been done in terms of rate of return measures, and a substitute measure would only be justifiable if it were a better measure. The *BK* ratio being a straightforward transformation of the relevant *SER* measure cannot be a better measure of social profitability than the rate of return measures. We will therefore not consider it as a serious contender for adoption as a general project selection procedure.

Table II: Goods and Factor Prices

	Goods			Factors	
	X	M	N	L	K
I. *Protection*					
Prices	eP_{xf}	$eP_{mf(2+t)}$	P_n	W	R
II. *Free Trade P_n Fixed and Variable Exchange Rate*					
Prices	e^*P_{xf}	e^*P_{mf}	P_n	W^*	R^*

Note: e — is the exchange rate.
  P_{xf} — the foreign currency price of X (the exportable).
  P_{mf} — the foreign currency price of M (the importable).
  P_n — the price of the nontraded good N.
  R — the rental rate on capital (K).
  W — the wage rate paid to labor (L).

Third, there is the *Little-Mirrlees procedure.* This method takes foreign currency as its numeraire, values tradeable inputs and outputs[14] at their border prices (c.i.f. price if an importable, f.o.b. if an exportable)[15] and those of nontradeables as the *MSC* of production determined by breaking down the costs of production into tradeables and primary factors. The former then being valued at border prices and the latter by revaluing the domestic currency value marginal product of these factors in terms of foreign exchange. It can be used on both the alternative assumptions that existing trade restrictions are going to continue, as well as on the alternative assumption that there will be future trade-liberalization. As we have seen in terms of the simple models outlined above,

(1) If the protection structure is assumed to remain unchanged, the *LM* method gives equivalent social rankings of investment projects as the *UHS SER* method. The same adjustments are required in the relative prices of traded goods, which on both the *LM* and *UHS* procedures will be equal to their "border" relative prices. For nontraded goods and primary factors the *LM* method would estimate specific conversion factors. For primary factors these would be the ratio of the *VMP* in domestic to that in foreign currency in the *protection* situation, while for nontraded goods it would be given by revaluing the *MSC* of production in foreign exchange to obtain the "shadow" price of the nontraded good in foreign exchange, and the ratio of the market to "shadow" price would then be the conversion factor for the nontraded good. On the *UHS* method in contrast, an average conversion factor (the *SER)* would be worked out to convert foreign currency values of traded goods into "domestic currency" values.

(2) If trade liberalization is assumed, with the price of nontraded goods fixed, but a flexible exchange rate, the *LM* method would give equivalent social rankings of investment projects as the *BT* method. The *LM* method would take the foreign prices of tradeables as their shadow prices, and work out the implicit prices of the nontraded goods and factors in the *free trade* situation in terms of foreign exchange equivalents, *implicitly* at the free trade "equilibrium" exchange rate, which is the *BT SER.* The correct application of the *BT SER* method would involve obtaining the shadow prices of the traded goods by multiplying their foreign currency values by the *BT SER.* The shadow prices of the nontraded goods would be their market prices in the protection situation (as *ex hypothesi* the prices of nontraded goods are

---

[14]As noted above, it is assumed in this section that trade distortions are in the form of tariffs; import quota restrictions are considered in the section headed *Quantitative Restrictions.*
[15]If the country is a monopolist/monopsonist, in foreign trade for any good, then the relevant border prices are the marginal revenue/cost in exporting/importing the good.

inflexible),[16] and the factor prices would be the domestic money prices of the factors which would exist under free trade. The latter are clearly needed by both the *LM* and *BT SER* methods.

Thus, there are essentially two basic methods of project appraisal (with two variants for each, depending upon the particular assumptions made about future trade liberalization), namely the *domestic currency as numeraire, SER methods,* and the *foreign currency as numeraire, LM methods.* In principle as we have shown the two types of methods involve nothing more than a change in numeraire. In practice, however, there are certain advantages in using the *LM* (foreign currency as numeraire) methods rather than the *SER* (domestic currency as numeraire) methods in a relatively open economy. The next section discusses these issues.

LM and SER Procedures in Practice[17]

The relative advantage in a relatively open economy of using the *LM* procedures rather than the *SER* ones, *in practice,* depends essentially upon its estimation and use of multiple conversion factors for converting nontraded goods and primary factors (domestic currency items) into foreign currency (the *LM* numeraire), in contrast with the *SER* procedures which use a *single* conversion factor, an *SER,* for converting foreign currency into domestic currency (the *SER* method's numeraire).

Note that (as we have emphasized) in *principle* both methods require the same information, and merely involve a change in numeraire. Thus to compare the two methods, it is simplest to abstract from this change by working for the moment in the same numeraire, say, *foreign currency,* to see the differing prescriptions *in practice* on the two procedures. As we saw in Numerical Examples 1 and 2, both methods would take the relative prices of traded goods to be their border prices, and as we are taking foreign currency as the numeraire, these would be the border prices in foreign currency. This leaves the problem of converting various "domestic currency" items (nontraded goods, primary factors and domestically produced tradeables) into foreign currency equivalents. If, as in the first case of Numerical Example 1, we use

---

[16]In general, the movement to a new free trade equilibrium from the protection situation could entail a combined change in the price of the nontraded good and the exchange rate. The *BT SER* would then have to correspond to this particular free trade exchange rate, and it will also be necessary to determine the change in the price of the nontraded good. However, as in the final free trade equilibrium, the domestic money relative prices of all goods will be the same on either the variable exchange rate and fixed nontraded good price or fixed exchange rate and flexible nontraded good price, adjustment process, the relative factor prices will be the same. Hence on the *LM* procedures there will be no need to make any further estimates than these given in the text. See Lal [17].

[17]This chapter has been considerably improved by the written comments of Maurice Scott on an earlier draft.

a single conversion factor (the inverse of an *SER*) to make the conversions, then the two methods *LM* and *SER* are also *identical in practice*. However, as was emphasized in the second case of Numerical Example 1, this process involves averaging across a multiplicity of actual (implicit) effective rates of exchange. The derivation of an average single conversion factor on *SER* lines, as opposed to the estimation and use of the actual multiple conversion factors on *LM* lines then creates two types of problems in practice for the *SER* method.

The first is of *accuracy,* and the second the *ease* with which the exercise can be done. Any process of averaging must to some extent be arbitrary. As we saw in the second case in Numerical Example 1, the estimate of the *UHS SER* depended crucially upon the weights α and β. There is some doubt whether conceptually the weights which are recommended are the right ones to use in an economy which uses imported intermediate goods subject to differentiated tariffs or quotas or both.[18] While even if this were clear, it is not easy in practice to determine these weights. Finally, often the goods over which the averaging is to be done is also not clear. Thus in many cases in deriving an *SER,* all locally produced items, even if they are tradeable, are counted as domestic currency items, and even though their relative domestic prices are very different from their relative border prices. An *SER* derived by treating these goods as nontraded (and implicitly with their relative domestic prices assumed to measure their relative marginal contributions to aggregate consumption) could be a misleading parameter. These difficulties in determining in practice the goods over which the averaging should be done and estimating the weights to be employed to obtain the single *SER,* show up in the widely divergent estimates of the *SER* which are made for the same country.[19] The *SER* can thus be a very slippery concept and treacherous parameter. The main advantage of the *LM* procedures is that by using multiple conversion factors, they cut through this problem of deriving a *single* conversion factor (an *SER*). They will thus be both more accurate and easier to apply in practice.

It should be noted that there is one conversion factor determined on *LM* procedures which (at least conceptually) is closely analogous to an *SER,* namely the *LM* conversion factor for marginal consumption expenditures,[20] which is normally estimated as part of the estimation process of determining the shadow wage rate. This conversion factor can also be estimated and

[18]See fn. 9 in this chapter.

[19]Maurice Scott reports that he has seen estimates for Pakistan "which ranged from a premium of 25 to 100 or more percent over the official rate." While for India recent estimates of the *UHS SER* range from Beyer's [3] estimates of US \$1 = Rs 9.8 to 10.3, to Dasgupta's [5] estimates of Rs 16.50 to Rs 21.00 (the official exchange rate is Rs 7.5 to US \$1), implying premiums of 30 to 180 percent over the official rate.

[20]See p. 12f.

used to value any consumption foregone in cases where the basic assumptions of the *LM* procedures that the effects of the project are directly and/or indirectly on domestic production and trade are not justified.[21] But it should be noted that in practice on the *LM* method there could be a multiplicity of these consumption conversion factors, depending upon the groups which are affected and their pattern of expenditure. If a conversion factor for aggregate consumption, namely the ratio of the domestic to the foreign exchange cost of a marginal change in aggregate consumption, is derived, this would be closely analogous to the *SER* determined on *UHS* lines. While the use of such a consumption conversion factor (or factors) is clear-cut on the *LM* method, the use of this same (or similar) single conversion factor for converting all the domestic currency items into foreign currency ones (or vice versa) on the *SER* method, when there are a multiplicity of conversion factors for primary factors and nontraded goods in an economy with both tradeable and nontraded intermediate goods, and with a highly differentiated tariff structure, is by no means clear.

If, of course, on the *domestic currency as numeraire methods,* the *LM* practice of decomposing nontraded goods into their tradeable goods and primary factor components; of counting domestically produced tradeable goods as "foreign currency" items; and of determining the consequent multiple conversion factors for nontraded goods and primary factors were also followed, then the two methods would be identical. There would be an *LM* consumption conversion factor (for aggregate consumption) to be used specifically for converting particular consumption changes, which would be like an *SER,* but the general method would *be* the *LM* method.[22]

Finally, there are obvious diplomatic advantages in not having to calculate a specific factor labeled the *SER,* as governments are not likely to take kindly to the calculation (and publication) of a "shadow" exchange rate for their countries.

Quantitative Restrictions (QR)

In the analysis of trade distortions, we have so far assumed that they were in the form of unchanging tariffs and subsidies. In practice, however, most developing countries make extensive use of *QR's* along with tariffs. This considerably complicates the task of project evaluators. The correct shadow

---

[21]See page 12 f.

[22]This has been explicitly stated by *LM:* "We have certainly seen project analyses where all nontraded purchases (in practice often called local purchases) are lumped together, and a single conversion factor applied. So we believe that the main superiority of the *Manual* is that it advocates the use of many exchange rates. If in fact UNIDO does the same, the differences between the two approaches could, we believe, be set dancing on the head of a pin." Little and Mirrlees [25], p. 163.

price of a good subject to a QR will depend upon how the QR regime is operated. (1) In one limiting case, *the QR's could be operated in a manner equivalent to a tariff,* whereby the full impact of any increased supply or demand for the good subject to a QR is on trade. Thus, if there was an increase in demand for the good, the QR would be relaxed, and conversely if there was increased domestic supply of the good. In this case, the same considerations we have discussed in the model exclusively with tariffs, would be relevant in determining the shadow price of the goods. (2) The other limiting case would be where the QR *is rigidly fixed,* so that the impact of increased demand and supply of the good subject to a QR is purely on domestic consumption and production. In this case the good subject to a rigid import quota will be equivalent to a nontraded good (the government having implicitly charged an infinite tax or transportation charge on the importable after a certain level of imports). Once again, in this case the methods of evaluation will be identical to the methods for valuing nontraded goods on the alternative procedures discussed previously. (3) The difficult problems arise in intermediate cases where the working of the QR regime falls between these two limiting cases. Then the increased use or production of the good subject to a QR may in part be on trade, in part on domestic production and in part on domestic consumption. For such *partially traded* goods, say an increase in demand is met from all three sources. The social cost of meeting this demand will then just be the weighted average of the social costs of a marginal increase in domestic production, decrease in domestic consumption and increase (decrease) in imports (exports) of the good; the weights being the estimates of the proportionate share of these alternative sources in meeting the increase in demand. The proportion which comes from foreign trade is valued on the LM procedures as a traded good, and that which comes from domestic production as a nontraded good. This leaves the proportion which comes from domestic consumption. The effect of the increased demand for the partially traded good would have led to some bidding up of its domestic price, and hence the switching of consumer expenditure away from it to other goods and services. The accounting cost in foreign exchange of providing these alternative goods and services to consumers, will then be the social cost of obtaining the good from domestic consumption for use on the project; that is the aggregate consumption conversion factor can be used to revalue the proportion of the project's demand which is met, from reduced domestic consumption of the good. Thus if, say, Rs a worth of the good is obtained from reduced domestic consumption then the social costs will just be $$a \cdot y$ (where y is the consumption conversion factor defined as the foreign exchange equilavent of providing Rs 100 of consumption).[23] Clearly for goods which bulk large in the costs and benefits

---

[23]See p. 12 f.

of a particular project, and which are subject to this intermediate type of *QR* system, it will be necessary to derive the shadow price on the above principle for each individual case. However, for a majority of goods subject to such controls, and which do not form an important part of the cost-benefits of the project, it will be impractical to make such detailed calculations for each and every input and output. Shortcuts, as well as practical guidelines, then become essential. The *LM* procedures suggest that for such partially traded goods, the general assumption, except for important cases, should be that they are treated as fully as traded goods, if the quotas are worked closer to the flexible *QR* type of regime, and as nontraded goods, if they are worked to correspond to a rigid quota type of *QR* regime.

The UNIDO system, on the other hand, apart from stating the theoretical principle, does not provide any general guidelines for such goods. Nevertheless, the existence of such goods and of *QR's* poses severe problems for both the UNIDO and *BT* methods in the computations of their respective *SER's*. For in general it is not possible to deduce the tariff equivalent of a quota from the ratio of domestic and foreign prices of the relevant good. And as it is these implicit or explicit tariff rates, or both, which appear in the *BT* and *UHS SER's*, it is extremely difficult to provide a general formula for the *SER's* under a quota regime, and even more importantly to obtain the necessary information for computing them accurately.

Summing Up

Thus, summing up this discussion of the relevant merits of alternative procedures for taking account of trade distortion, clearly the *first* crucial judgment is with regard to the future trade control system. If it is assumed to remain unchanged, then the *UHS SER* or the *LM* procedure, which assumes protection remains unchanged, is appropriate. If trade liberalization is assumed to occur, then the *BT SER* and the *LM* procedure which assumes trade liberalization will be appropriate. The difference lies in judgments about whether the relevant prices are the shadow prices corresponding to the *MSC's* and *MSV's* in the protection situation, or the "equilibrium" prices corresponding to the free trade situation. There may be something to be said for doing calculations on both sets of assumptions.

Second, as regards comparisons of the relative merits of using *LM* or *SER* procedures, we have shown that *in principle,* they are equivalent, involving no more than a change in numeraire. They require the same information. *In practice,* however, *LM* methods could be more accurate and also easier to apply than *SER* ones in economies with a highly differentiated tariff structure and hence a multiplicity of effective exchange rates, for converting "domestic" into "foreign" currency values. Moreover, the derviation of an average of these multiple conversion factors in the form of a single *SER* is subject to all the difficulties (conceptual as well as operational) involved in any process of averaging. Widely divergent *SER's* may then be (and have been) calculated for the same country.[24] Hence there may be practical advantages in using the *LM* methods instead of *SER* ones.

Finally, there are obvious diplomatic advantages in the *LM* procedures in not having to estimate a parameter (a shadow exchange rate) which is considered to be such a politically sensitive issue in many developing countries.

---

[24]See footnote 19 in this chapter.

II. Distortions in Factor Markets

In this part we relax the assumption made in Chapter I that factor markets are perfectly competitive. We now introduce factor market distortions but, for simplicity and clarity, assume away all other distortions. Thus the domestic market prices of the two primary factors will no longer be taken to equal their *social* opportunity costs, as we had hitherto assumed. Distortions in both the markets for labor and capital have been discussed in the project evaluation literature. The two fully fledged evaluation procedures, the UNIDO and *LM* procedures, identify the same distortions and, except for some differences in assumptions about the likely future changes in some of the divergences, provide identical rules in principle, except for a difference in numeraire. The UNIDO procedures take current consumption as their numeraire, the *LM* current savings.[1] Note that current savings generate the time stream of future consumption. As consumption, following the practice in theoretical welfare economics, is identified as the source of economic welfare, this means that the net benefits will be dated consumption, and there will be the problem of making commensurable present consumption and future consumption. As long as the same relative price between present and future consumption is used to "add up" the intertemporal net benefits of the project, it does not matter which of the two relevant "commodities" (present consumption or future consumption [savings]), we take as our numeraire.[2]

---

[1]More precisely the *LM* numeraire is "uncommitted social income measured at border prices." It need not be saved, but could be spent on uses (like administration, health, law and order, et cetera) which are considered as useful as savings by the government.

[2]The only difference will be the "cosmetic" one that the appropriate discount rate to be used with savings as the numeraire will generally be *higher* than that to be used with consumption as the numeraire. See equation (7) below, which gives the relationship between the two discount rates.

We turn first to examine the adjustments necessary to take account of the distortions in the market for capital.

Capital

Savings and investment are the means for changing the time shape of the intertemporal consumption stream which is feasible given resource and technological transformation constraints. The capital market intermediates between those making savings and investment decisions. In a perfect capital market, the social return from one unit of current savings (the net present value of the consumption stream made possible by one unit of current savings) at the margin, is equal to the social value of one unit of current consumption. The former will depend upon the opportunities open to society in production, to convert one unit of present consumption into future consumption—that is, the social productivity of investment—the latter on the weight society places on one unit of future consumption in terms of present consumption—the social rates of time preference. In a perfect capital market, the rate of interest R will equal and equate the marginal rate of transformation (mrt) of present into future consumption, and the marginal rate of indifferent substitution (mrs) of present and future consumption. That is $R = mrt = mrs$, of the two "commodities" present and future consumption. Distortions in the capital market will drive a wedge between the components of the above marginal equivalence, so that $mrt \neq mrs$. Moreover, the rate of interest may not equal either the mrt or mrs. Furthermore, if the capital market is segmented, there may be a multiplicity of rates of interest.

Two basic sources of distortions have been identified as causing the divergence between the mrt and mrs of present and future consumption. One is due to the presence of externalities, the other to the presence of monopolistic or fiscal distortions or both in the capital market. We will consider the causes and adjustments for the former type of distortion, the causes of the latter type being self-evident, and the remedies being similar to those suggested for the former type.

The source of the externality in the capital market is due to the interdependence and the mortality of private savers. Being mortal, they cannot be expected to extend their altruism to the infinite generations which are properly the concern of a society, which at least in principle, is immortal. As a result, the savings (future consumption) generated, *ceteris paribus,* as a result of the decisions of private savers is likely to be less than socially optimal. Furthermore, *if* private savers knew that everyone else was going to save at the socially optimal rate, then they too would agree to save at this rate. Hence, the externality. The result is that the private rate of time preference is higher than the social. Under laissez faire, a perfect capital market would insure that enough savings would be invested until the social return to investment (savings) fell to the private rate of time preference. That is the private marginal rate of substitution *(mrs_p)* in consumption would be equated to the private and *ex hypothesi, social,* marginal rate of transformation *(mrt)* in production, of present into future consumption. However, as the externality causes the marginal *private* rate of substitution to be higher than the marginal *social* rate of substitution *(mrs)*, we have $mrs_p = mrt > mrs$.

Once again the first best solution would be to cure the above divergence, by appropriate tax-subsidy policy; in this case by using fiscal policy to raise the savings rate in the economy till *mrs_p* and *mrt* had become equal to *mrs*. Note that as the savings level is raised toward the optimal level, *mrs* will rise and *mrs_p* and *mrt* will fall.

However, the government may have imperfect control over savings in the economy, and may not be able to legislate the optimal savings rate by direct fiscal means. In that case, it will be necessary to take account of the divergence in the *mrt* and *mrs* in the capital market. As long as the divergence exists, current savings are socially more valuable than current consumption. Hence, if the government can indirectly, through its choice of projects, influence the savings rate, this "savings constraint" may be overcome over time till savings and consumption are considered to be equally socially valuable. The way in which the government could influence the savings-consumption balance of the economy through project choice is by influencing the choice of techniques and by choosing projects whose benefits tend to be saved and reinvested rather than consumed.

The way in which both the UNIDO and *LM* procedures take account of the divergence is by differentially weighting the project's net benefits which are consumed and those which are saved. *The only difference between the procedures in principle is the difference in numeraires.* Whereas (a) the UNIDO procedures use *present consumption* as the numeraire, and put a *premium on savings,* (b) the *LM* procedures use *current savings* as the numeraire, and *penalize consumption.* To see this, consider the following simple algebraic example.

Algebraic Example: First, consider the procedure adopted in the UNIDO *Guidelines,* which takes *consumption as its numeraire.* Assume that the net benefits from a project in any year *(t)* are *Bt,* and that of these ϴ percent in any year are saved and reinvested and $(1 - ϴ)$ percent are consumed. The social rate of time preference today is d_o, and the social return to investment today is r_o $(r_o > d_o)$. Moreover, over time the divergence between *r* and *d* is likely to diminish, till *T* years from today the divergence will disappear (the level of savings will be optimal). Finally, the project incurs capital costs of *K* in the base year, yielding the stream of net benefits for *N* years.

To obtain the social profitability of the project we first note that the opportunity cost of the capital costs K is the present value of the future consumption which would have resulted if Rs K of present investment were made at the current social rate of return to investment, r_0. Thus, if Rs 1 of current investment, which is assumed to remain intact forever, leads to net output of Rs 1.1 in the next period, $r_0 = 1.1/1 = .1$. Part of this return (Θ) will be saved and invested. Hence, the increase in investment next year ($t = 1$) will be $[1 \ (1 + r_0) - 1] \Theta = r_0 \Theta$. Total investment next year will therefore be $(1 + r_0 \Theta)$. The year after next ($t = 2$) investment will increase by $[(1 + r_0 \Theta) (1 + r_1) - (1 + r_0\Theta)] \Theta = (1 + r_0 \Theta) r_1 \Theta$. Total investment in year $t = 2$ will therefore be $[(1 + r_0 \Theta) r_1 y \Theta + (1 + r_0 \Theta)] = (1 + r_0\Theta) (1 + r_1 \Theta)$. Hence, by year T, when the savings constraint ceases to operate, total investment would have accumulated to: $(1 + r_0 \Theta) \ (1 + r_1 \Theta) \ldots (1 + r_{T-1} \Theta)$. To get the present value of this accumulated investment which, *ex hypothesi*, is as valuable as an equal amount of consumption at T, we have to discount its value back to the present ($t = 0$) at the changing social rates of time preference ($d_0, d_1, d_2 \ldots d_T$), period by period. This present value is:

$$(1 + r_0 \Theta) (1 + r_1 \Theta) \ldots (1 + r_{T-1} \Theta)/$$
$$(1 + d_1) (1 + d_2) \ldots (1 + d_T) \qquad (1)$$

In addition to this accumulated investment, the initial Rs 1 of investment will have resulted in consumption of $(1 - \Theta) (1 + r_0 \Theta)$ in $t = 1$; of $(1 - \Theta) (1 + r_0 \Theta) (1 + r_1 \Theta)$ in $t = 2$; and hence in year t of $(1 - \Theta) (1 + r_0 \Theta) (1 + r_1 \Theta) \ldots (1 + r_{t-1} \Theta)$. The present value of this stream of consumption is:

$$\sum_{t=0}^{T} \frac{(1 - \Theta) (1 + r_0 \Theta) \ldots (1 + r_{t-2} \Theta) (1 + r_{t-1} \Theta)}{(1 + d_1) \ldots (1 + d_{t-1}) \ (1 + d_t)} \qquad (2)$$

Confining our time horizon to T, the present value of the stream of consumption made possible by Rs 1 of investment today (s_0) is then:

$$s_0 = (1) + (2) \qquad (3)$$

The social opportunity costs of capital expenditure of K today are therefore $s_0 K$.

The benefits are B_t in year (t), of which ΘB_t will be saved and invested. The value of this savings in terms of consumption at date t will be given by the social opportunity cost of investment in year t, which on an analogous argument to that for deriving s_0, will be s_t. The rest of the benefits $(1 - \Theta) B_t$ will be consumed in year t. Hence, the present value of the stream of net benefits will be given by:

$$\sum_{t=0}^{N} \frac{(1 - \Theta) B_t + s_t \Theta B_t}{(1 + d_1) (1 + d_2) \ldots (1 + d_t)} \qquad (4)$$

and the *NPV* of the project will be given by:

$$NPV = (4) - s_0 K \qquad (5)$$

27

Thus on the "generalized" UNIDO procedures[3] it is necessary to know both the changing social return to investment (the r_t's) as well as the changing social rates of discount (the d_t's). Moreover, the discount rate used to obtain the NPV of the project will be the social discount rates d_t's.

The alternative *LM procedure* takes *savings as its numeraire,* and uses the own rate of return on investment (called the accounting rate of interest, *ARI*) as the discount rate. However, as we will show, it is identical to the "generalized" UNIDO procedures, except for the change in numeraire. Following the same argument as before, and making the same assumptions, we found that Rs 1 of investment yielded a present value of total future consumption generated by the investment of s_0. That is, Rs 1 of current savings (investment) is worth s_0 of present consumption. Consumption therefore has $(1/s_0)$ the value if the same resources had been invested. In year 1, therefore, the value of $(1 - \Theta)(1 + r_0 \Theta)$ consumption generated is $(1 - \Theta)(1 + r_0 \Theta)/s_1$. In year t, the value of the consumption generated from the net benefits of the project will be $B_t(1 - \Theta)/s_t$.

In each year there will also be yB_t savings generated, and these will be valuable at par, as savings is our numeraire. The total value, in terms of savings of the net benefits in any year, will then be:
$$B_t(1 - \Theta)/s_t + \Theta B_t.$$
These total savings benefits in each year have then to be discounted back to the present at the accounting rate of interest, *(ARI) (p_t)*[4] in each period to get the present savings value of the project. Hence, the NPV of the project on the *LM* procedures will be given by:
$$NPV = \sum_{t=0}^{N} \frac{B_t(1 - \Theta)/s_t + \Theta B_t}{(1 - p_1) \ldots (1 + p_{t-1})(1 + p_t)} - K \qquad (6)$$
Note that as savings is our numeraire, the capital costs K, incurred in year 0 are valued at par.

Moreover, the *LM Manual* derives a relationship between p_t, s_t, and d_t. It is:
$$s_t/s_{t+1} = (1 + p_t)/(1 + d_t) \qquad (7)$$

---

[3]"Generalized" because, as the next section explains, the way in which s is calculated on the UNIDO *Guidelines* assumes that its value remains constant over time. This, in practice, is likely to be an implausible assumption. But as the above account suggests, the UNIDO approach can be generalized, so that it is identical to the *LM* one, except for the change in numeraire.

[4]Thus, if say Rs 1 of investment today leads to a net return of Rs 0.1 tomorrow, of which half (.05) is saved and invested, and if consumption has no social value in terms of the numeraire savings, then the *ARI* is .05/1 = .05. If on the other hand, consumption and savings are considered socially equally valuable, then the *ARI* would be .1/1 = 0.1. In general if the value of one unit of consumption in terms of savings is $1/s$, the *ARI* in this example will be $(.05 + .05/s)$.

28

Now *consider a two period case,* that is from $t = 0$ to $t - 1$. For the project to be acceptable *on the LM criterion,* the *NPV* given by (6) should be positive, that is:

$$\frac{B_1[(1 - \Theta)(1/s_1) + \Theta]}{(1 + p_1)} \geq K \tag{8}$$

Multiplying both sides of (8) by s_1, and then dividing both sides by $s \sqrt{s_0}$, we get:

$$\frac{B_1[(1 - \Theta) + \Theta s_1]}{s_1/s_0 \cdot (1 + p_1)} \geq s_0 K \tag{9}$$

From (7) the denominator of the *LHS* of (9) is equal to $(1 + d_1)$, hence, we get (9) equal to:

$$\frac{B_1[(1 - \Theta) + \Theta s_1]}{(1 + d_1)} \geq s_0 K \tag{10}$$

as the criterion for accepting a project on the *LM* procedure.

But now consider the same two period case *on the UNIDO procedures;* the acceptance criterion is that the *NPV* given by (5) be positive; and it can be seen from (4) and (5) that this gives the identical result (10) as the criterion of acceptability. *Hence, the two procedures LM and UNIDO are identical* in terms of the information needed to take account of suboptimal savings. The differences in the discount rates on the two procedures (the *ARI* on the *LM,* the social rate of discount on the UNIDO) *merely reflect a change in numeraire.*

LM and UNIDO in Practice: To show the equivalence *in principle* of the two procedures, in the above algebraic example, we had assumed that the value of s is calculated on the UNIDO procedures *on the LM assumption* that savings and consumption will be equally valuable T years from today. *In practice,* however, the formula given by UNIDO to calculate the value of s assumes that the divergence in the relative social value of aggregate consumption and savings, and hence the value of s *remains constant* till infinity. Thus the UNIDO formula for calculating s is:

$$s = (1 - \Theta) r/(d - \Theta r),$$

where y = marginal propensity to save,
r = rate of return on investment, and
d = social rate of discount of consumption.

(See UNIDO [32], p. 175 onwards.) This equation will only provide meaningful values if $d > \Theta r$, otherwise the social value of investment (s) will be infinite (see UNIDO [32], p. 189). There is no plausible economic reason why d must necessarily be greater than Θr.[5] Moreover, the actual value of s given by the formula will be very sensitive to the values chosen for d, Θ

---

[5] Thus Maurice Scott points out that "one could argue that d should be zero in Mauritius (with per capita consumption roughly constant) while y and r are both positive."

and r, and small differences in the values of these variables could lead to large differences in the value of s.

The assumption of a constant divergence in the relative social values of aggregate consumption and savings, and hence a constant s must therefore be rejected in favor of the more plausible *LM* assumption that this divergence disappears after T years and hence s will typically fall over time to a value of unity at T.[6]

Finally, it should be emphasized that both procedures require information on the social rate of discount and the social rate of return to investment in the economy. We therefore next examine how these parameters can be estimated.

Estimating the Intertemporal Parameters:[7] The *LM Manual* gives a formula[8] relating the ARI_0 (p_0), and the social discount rate (d_0) to s_0 and T. This is:
$$s_0 = [1 + \tfrac{1}{2} (p_0 - d_0)]^T \tag{11}$$
Given the definition of the *ARI*:
$$p_0 = r_0 [\Theta + (1 - \Theta)/s_0] \tag{12}$$
Hence, substituting (12) into (11) we have:
$$s_0 = \left\{ 1 + \tfrac{1}{2} [r_0 (\Theta + (1 - \Theta) / s_0) - d_0] \right\}^T \tag{13}$$
This formula succinctly expresses the various intertemporal parameters we need to estimate. These are r_0, d_0, T and Θ; and given these s_0 will be determined.

The social return to investment is r_0 and Θ is the percentage of this return saved; r_0 will thus be the return at accounting prices from marginal current investments. On certain plausible assumptions,[9] this return can be derived as a weighted average of social rates of profits on existing investments in the economy. Θ, can be estimated from data on savings propensities and tax rates.

This leaves d_0, the social discount rate, and T the date when savings and consumption are expected to be equally valuable, to be estimated.

The social discount rates (d_t) reflect the distributional weighting given to income (consumption) transfers between generations. In determining these weights it is plausible to assume that as a result of the normal processes of growth, future generations will in any case be richer than present ones. Just

---

[6]Another consequence of assuming a constant s $(s_t = s_{t+1})$ is that from (7) above the discount rate $(p_t = d_t)$ is the same on both *LM* and UNIDO procedures.

[7]A fuller discussion is contained in Lal [22].

[8]See Little and Mirrlees [25], p. 179, and Lal [21], Appendix II.

[9]See Lal [22] for the derivation of such a rate from a heterogenous capital dual economy model which avoids the capital theoretic problems arising for derivations based on aggregate production functions. This method is also similar to that advocated by Harberger; see his *Project Evaluation: Collected Papers*. Chicago: Markham, 1972. For an application of the method, see Lal [21], Appendix II.

how much richer will depend upon the expected rate of growth per capita consumption over the future. Suppose the latter rate is g. Further assume that the elasticity of social marginal utility (defined as the percentage change in social utility resulting from a percentage change in consumption), with respect to per capita changes in consumption is e. Then it can be shown[10] that

$$d_t = (1 + g_t)^e - 1 \qquad (14)$$

This leaves T, which is rather harder to determine. However, from projections of expected growth rates of national income and savings, it may be possible to arrive at some estimate of the likely date by which savings are likely to be sufficient to give an adequate long term growth rate. This date can then be taken to be T.

Labor[11]

One of the most common forms of distortion identified in the project evaluation literature is in the labor markets of surplus labor economies, such that the wage rate does not equal the social opportunity cost of labor in the economy.

Two components have been traditionally identified in the social opportunity cost of labor in surplus labor economies. The *first* is the output foregone elsewhere in the economy, as a result of employing labor on the project. The *second* are the costs in terms of increased aggregate consumption that may result as more labor (which consumes most of its income) is employed on the project. If, due to the nonoptimality of savings (discussed above) present consumption is socially less valuable than current savings, then any increase in aggregate consumption, caused by increasing employment as a result of the project, will not be as valuable as the equivalent amount of savings. This factor will have to be reflected in the measure of the social opportunity cost of labor.

To concretize this, consider a particular formulation of the social opportunity cost of labor, that is the shadow wage rate *(SWR)* due to *LM*. Except for a change in numeraire, which *LM* take to be "savings" rather than consumption, their analysis is similar to other well-known ones due to Sen and Marglin, and which have been incorporated in the UNIDO procedures.

Assume first that the wage paid to a laborer in his new job, c, is above the value of the output foregone elsewhere by moving him from his previous employment, m. Second, given the nonoptimality of savings, and taking savings as the numeraire, one unit of current consumption is socially worth

---

[10]Assuming a constant elasticity social utility function (U) which has per capita consumption (C) as one of its arguments, then $U = C^e$, and $d_t = (U_t^1/U_{t+1}^1)C$, and $g = (C_{t+1} - C_t)/C_t$. Hence $d_t = (1 + g)^e - 1$.

[11]This section is based on Lal [18], where a fuller treatment of the subject may be found.

$(1/s)$ units of current savings. *The s factor is the same as in the discussion of capital* in the previous section. Then, the costs of employing one more person in the economy (in terms of savings) are given by:

$$SWR = m + (c - m) - (c - m)/s \qquad (15)$$

The first term on the *RHS* is the output foregone elsewhere in the economy, which has been traditionally identified with the marginal product of labor in agriculture. In addition, assuming that workers in both industry and agriculture consume all their incomes, the economy will be committed to providing them with extra consumption of $(c - m)$ as $c > m$. This increase in aggregate consumption must be at the expense of aggregate savings given the well-known Keynesian national income identities. But given the non-optimality of savings, this increase in aggregate consumption (decrease in savings) must represent a social cost. As, *ex hypothesi,* society values s units of consumption as equal in social value to one unit of savings, the net social cost of the increase in consumption (in terms of the numeraire, savings) will be

$$(c - m) - (c - m)s$$

which are the second and third terms of (15). The above expression reduces to:

$$SWR = c - (c - m)/s \qquad (16)$$

We now turn to the determination of the output foregone $(m),$ and various other complications in determining the *SER,* in the following sections.

Output Foregone: In most conventional analyses the output foregone $m,$ in the above *SWR* formulation, has been identified with the marginal product of the relevant labor in its previous employment. While this would, given certain other assumptions to be discussed, be correct for labor which was previously in wage employment, it may not in general be correct for labor which was previously self-employed. This is an important consideration, in view of the fact that in most developing countries a substantial portion of the labor force is self-employed.

Moreover, in most conventional analyses it was also assumed that the marginal product of the laborer withdrawn from the traditional sector, agriculture, would be zero and hence $m = 0$. In a definitive analysis of dualism and surplus labor within a model of family farms on which there is equal work and income sharing, and which explicitly incorporated leisure as an argument in the individual peasant's utility function, Sen [28] demonstrated that zero marginal productivity was not a necessary condition for the existence of surplus labor. The necessary and sufficient conditions being given by a constant disutility of effort, which implies a constant marginal rate of substitution between income and leisure over the relevant range of hours worked per man, in the traditional sector. Given this, output in the traditional sector would not fall with the withdrawal of workers, and hence for them $m = 0,$

even though the marginal productivity of labor was positive in the traditional sector. Thus, in general, for a family farm worker withdrawn from a farm without any hired labor, the change in output will not equal his marginal product.

Divergence Between Average and Marginal Costs: Certain writers have noted that the conventional analysis may *understate* the extra consumption cost of industrial labor. This is due to the assumption made in these analyses that "agricultural" workers can be hired by the "industrial" sector at a constant real wage *(Wi),* which is either given by a constant institutional wage, or else by a constant supply price of labor to the industrial sector. Dixit [7] suggests that this assumption may be unrealistic, especially if there are terms of trade effects following a withdrawal of labor from agriculture. Then, if the industrial labor market is competitive, the supply price of labor to industry and hence the industrial wage will rise with increased industrial employment.[12] This will create a divergence between the *average (c)* and *marginal (c + Δ c)* cost of hiring industrial labor. The extra consumption the economy will be committed to will then be given by the difference between the *marginal* cost of hiring *(c + Δ c)* and output foregone, *m.*[13]

---

[12]In the simple closed economy two-sector model analyzed by Dixit [7], the supply price of industrial labor is equal to the income foregone by agricultural family workers moving to industrial jobs. In short run equilibrium their income foregone is determined by the average physical product of labor in agriculture (assuming equal income sharing among family farm workers) and the relative price of agriculture output. With the withdrawal of an agricultural worker, the average product of labor in agriculture rises, while total agricultural output (assuming no surplus labor) falls. This last factor leads to a rise in the relative price of agricultural output. The net effect is to raise the average value product of labor in agriculture and hence the supply price of labor to the industrial sector.

[13]This can be seen heuristically from the accompanying diagram. *OI* is the industrial production function, with a given fixed capital stock and variable employment (*N*). The *OY* curve gives the total output foregone, and the *OWiN* curve the total wage bill for each level of industrial employment. The shape of both these curves reflects the assumed rising output foregone and wage rate (= agricultural income foregone) of industrial labor. Assume that there is an infinite premium on savings, and all wages are consumed. Social welfare is then maximized with the industrial employment level *ON**, where the marginal wage cost (slope of the tangent at *W*) is equal to the marginal product of labor (slope of the tangent at *P*). Hence to ensure the optimal level of industrial employment, a wage *tax* of *WS/ON** will have to be imposed. The slope of *OS* being equal to the slope of the tangent at *W*. The *SWR* is then given by $SN^*/ON^* = WN^* + WS = c + \Delta c.$

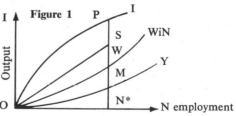

Figure 1

It is then easy to determine that when *s* > 1, but not infinite, the *SWR* will be given by expression (17) in the text, where *m* is also interpreted as the *marginal* output foregone.

Hence:
$$SWR = (c + \Delta c) - (c + \Delta c - m)/s \qquad (17)$$
and if the premium placed on savings is very high($s \to \infty$), the SWR will be higher than the market wage *(c)*. Note, however, that if there is a constant institutional wage in the industrial sector, then $c = 0$, and the SWR will be given as before by (16).

Rural-Urban Migration: As certain models of the labor market in developing countries have emphasized, the impact on net output in the economy cannot be deduced from the impact effects on output in the sector from which the new worker may be withdrawn. Hence, to obtain the value of *m,* it will be necessary to trace through all the indirect effects, in terms of the rural-urban migration that may ensue, as the result of creating one new job in, say, the industrial sector. Thus, if for instance we have say a laborer *A* moving to the project and his wage in his previous employment was \$*w,* and on his moving to the project his previous job is filled by someone else, *B,* who in turn moves from a job which paid him \$*Y (w > Y),* then the change in output (assuming that the two wage rates are determined in competitive markets for hired labor) by employing *A* on the project is not \$*w* but \$*Y,* as now the first round effect of *A's* migration—a fall of output of \$*w* in his previous employment—is offset by a rise in output in his previous activity by an equivalent amount when the other worker *B* replaced him, but which now results in the loss of output as a result of *B's* movement from his initial job to *A's* previous job of \$*Y.*

Furthermore, as a result of creating one more job in the "industrial" sector, more than one migrant may move from rural areas. If *N* people migrate, and the change in agricultural output as a result of one person's migration is *Y,* then the
$$SWR = c - (c - NY)/s \qquad (18)$$
Harberger [12] has used one particular model of rural-urban migration due to Harris-Todaro [14], to derive the SWR as always equal to the market wage *c*. This is obtained as follows. Harris-Todaro assume that there is *no* surplus labor in agriculture. The migrants come to the cities because the expected income in the urban sector is just equal to the income they forego in agriculture. The expected urban income is determined by the probability *(P)* of finding urban employment at the industrial wage *c,* which, in the Harris-Todaro model, is determined by the equilibrium ratio of employed to the total labor force in the cities, say *P*.[14] Furthermore, it is assumed that

---

[14]See Harris and Todaro [14], p. 128. This is also the assumption made by Harberger [11], p. 570. This formulation of *P* is unrealistic. A more likely determinant of the chances of a single migrant is given by the number of vacancies occuring per unit of time divided by the number of candidates for those vacancies, that is the urban unemployed. The latter in fact was the determinant of *P* in the earlier Todaro formulation

agricultural workers receive their marginal product (say a). At the margin, therefore, migrant workers will equate their marginal product (incomes) in agriculture, a, to the expected wage in towns, Pc (That is, $a = Pc$.) When one more man is hired by the industrial sector the expected wage Pc rises as P rises. This induces rural-urban migration of $1/P$ workers, which restores the probability of finding a job in the urban sector to P, and the expected income to the equilibrium level Pc—when rural-urban migration ceases. Hence in expression (18) $N = 1/P$. Morever, the "equilibrium" value of P is a/c (given the migration function $a = Pc$), and as the output foregone per migrant on Harris-Todaro assumptions is the marginal product a, we have:

$$m = NY = (1/P)a = c$$

Substitution in expressions (16) or (18) yields $SWR = c$, the industrial wage. However, as has been pointed out above, in general it cannot be assumed that the change in output in the agricultural sector will equal the marginal product of labor. In that case, the change in output m within the Harris-Todaro migration model will be given by Y/P, where Y is the change in output in agriculture when one worker is withdrawn. As before we have $a = Pc$ (where a is the income the worker received in agriculture, which on a family farm would be equal to the average product of the farm if we assume equal income and work sharing on family farms). Hence $m = Y/P = Y$. Then c/a and the SWR given a Harris-Todaro-type migration function will be:

$$SWR = c - c(1-Y/a)/s$$

From this it is obvious that, on the special Harris-Todaro assumption that $Y = a$, the SWR will equal c, the industrial wage. This is the Harberger derivation of the SWR, in his "Panama" example (see [12], p. 568 and following). More important, however, the Harris-Todaro-Harberger migration model is also restrictive in many other respects, some of which are more serious than others. First, it implicitly assumes that industrial wage-earners have tenure, as the rate of labor turnover in industry does not figure in their determination of P. Empirically, this assumption may not be too inaccurate, as the rate of labor turnover does not seem to be very high in the industrial sector in most developing countries. Second, they consider the migration decision as a one-period decision, whereas strictly it should be a multiperiod decision in which the present value of the costs of migration should at the

---

(see [31], p. 142). But note that while these differing determinants of P will affect the "equilibrium urban unemployment" rate (which is the chief concern of other writers on rural-urban migration), the *"equilibrium" value* of P will be invariant to these alternative formulations of its determinants, as it will be determined by the rural-urban income differential. (In our formulation above, the equilibrium $P = a/c$.) For a fuller discussion see Lal [18].

margin be equal to the present value of the benefits from migration.[15] If, however, as seems likely, most migrants have a fairly high subjective rate of time preference (fairly short time horizon), then the use of a single period migration decision function may not be invalid. Third, Harris-Todaro do not incorporate any of the costs of migration (real and/or "psychic")[16] nor the relatively higher costs of urban living which the migrant would have to incur in their migration function. Finally, and most important, their migration model fails to take account of the existence of a fairly competitive "unorganized" (services and small industry) sector urban labor market with high labor turnover and easy entry for new workers, which is typical of many developing countries, and which provides some income to the migrants while they are searching for an "organized" (industrial) sector job at the high institutional wage c.

Thus it is essentially the last two features which need to be incorporated into a more general migration function. To derive the SWR for this more general migration model, we continue to assume that industrial wage earners can be taken to have tenure, and that a one-period decision model is a fair approximation to reality. However, we now assume that in addition to the agricultural income foregone, a, the migrant has to incur migration costs of d, which include both the real and "psychic" costs of migrating. Furthermore, if the migrant does not succeed in obtaining an industrial sector job at the high institutional wage of c, he can nevertheless find some employment in the "unorganized" urban labor market and derive an income w. Finally, we assume that by living in the town the migrant has to incur a relatively higher cost of living than in rural areas of u to maintain the same standard of living as he enjoyed in the countryside. If the chances of getting an "organized" (industrial) sector job are as before P, then at the margin the migrant will equate the costs of migration, which are given by $(a + d + u)$ with the expected benefits, $[Pc + (1 - P)w]$, that is in equilibrium:

$$a + d + u = Pc + (1 - P)w.$$

This yields the "equilibrium" value of $P = (a + d + u - w)/(c - w)$.

As before, with the creation of an extra industrial sector job $N = 1/P$ migrants will move from agriculture, and as the output foregone per migrant in agriculture is Y, we have the total output foregone, $m = Y \cdot (c - w) / (a + d + u - w)$, and the

$$SWR = c - [c - Y \cdot (c - w) / (a + d + u - w)]/s \qquad (19)$$

and this more general and more realistic migration model, the conclusion drawn by Harberger that the institutionally given industrial wage c, is the shadow wage, will not be valid.

---

[15]Todaro [31], p. 143, fn. 10, notes this.

[16]Though Harris-Todaro note the existence of these costs, see their [14], p. 129, fn. 8.

Disutility of Effort: Finally, in addition to changes in output, there will also be changes in the aggregate disutility of effort (E) with increased employment. To evaluate these, assume initially that there are no imperfections in the labor market. Then, at the margin, utility maximizing workers will equate the disutility of increased effort with the utility from the increased incomes (which we assume are all consumed) this extra work makes possible. That is, the extra disutility of effort (E) must equal the change in workers' consumption (including those left behind on the farm) which is given by $(c - m)$—the difference between the industrial wage (assuming the new job is in industry, and the worker moves to it from agriculture) and the total output foregone by employing one more man in the industrial sector. The value in terms of savings of this change in disutility of effort (which so far is in terms of consumption equivalents) is $(c - m)/s$. If the value society places on the disutility of effort is λ, then the *SWR* incorporating the costs of the disutility of effort will be:

$$SWR = c - (c - m)/s + \lambda (c - m)/s$$
$$= c - (c - m)(1 - \lambda)/s \qquad (20)$$

Next relax the assumption that all labor markets are competitive, and assume that there is an institutional wage, c, in the sector to which the labor is moving which is above the supply price of labor L. The latter term includes all the private disutilities that may attach to the new job. Our earlier expression for the consumption equivalent of the net change in disutility $(c - m)$ will now be overstating the true change in disutility by $(c - L)$, which is the difference between the institutional wage c, and the supply price of labor L. The net change in disutilities in this more general case will therefore be given by $(c - m) - (c - L) = (L - m)$, and as before the value in terms of savings will be $(L - m)/s$, and the

$$SWR = c - (c - m)/s + \lambda (L - m)/s \qquad (21)$$

If λ = 0, that is society places no value on the change in the private disutilities of effort, we get the traditional *SWR* as in (16) above. If, however, it is assumed that society should value disutilities of effort at their private costs, then λ = 1, and the
$$SWR = L + (c - L)(1 - 1/s) \qquad (22)$$

The first term is the supply price of labor, the second is the value in terms of savings, of the extra consumption generated by the excess of the institutional wage over the supply price of labor. Thus, when λ = 1, we get the standard neoclassical result, that the *SWR* will be the supply price of labor, if there is no divergence between the social value of present consumption and savings, that is $s = 1$; and furthermore, that if $c = L$, that is, if labor markets are competitive, the *SWR* will equal the market wage c, no matter what the value

37

of s, and irrespective of any divergence between m (the output foregone elsewhere in the economy), and the industrial wage c.[17]

Alternative Formulations of the SWR: We can now, very succinctly, compare the various alternative *SWR's* that have been suggested in the literature.[18]

First, there is the view due to Galenson-Leibenstein [10] and Dobb [6] that the *SWR is the market wage,* that is *SWR* $= c$. For this to be the case, *either* $c = m = L$, or $m = 0, s \rightarrow \infty, \lambda = 0$, or $E = 0$.

Second, there is the view associated with Kahn [15] and Lewis [23] that the *SWR* $= 0$. For this to be the case: $m = 0, s = 1, \lambda = 0$, or $E = 0$.

Third, for Sen [29], Marglin [26] and to some extent UNIDO [32], the *SWR* $= c - c/s$. For this to be valid: $m = 0, \lambda = 0$, or $E = 0$.

Fourth, the *LM* [24] *SWR* is given by (16) above, *SWR* $= c - (c - m)/s$. For this to be valid: $\lambda = 0$. As they assume a positive marginal product in agriculture, E cannot be zero.

Finally, for Harberger [12], the *SWR is the supply price of labor L,* that is *SWR* $= L$. For this to be valid: either $\lambda = 1, c = L$, or $s = 1$.

Part of the differences relate to empirical matters, that is the value of m and E. But, in part, the differences relate to two value parameters, s and λ. The reasons why it may be necessary to take $s > 1$ have been given in the section

---

[17]Introducing rural-urban migration à la Harris-Todaro-Harberger, we know that with the employment of one extra worker in industry, $1/P$ workers will migrate, whose total supply price will be a/P (as a is the income foregone in agriculture by the migrating worker). Also if the output foregone per worker migrating from agriculture is Y, then the total output foregone with $1/P$ migrants is Y/P. We also have the equilibrium migration condition that $P = a/c$ (where c is the industrial wage), and we know from the above discussion that the net change in disutilities is given by the total supply price of labor and the output foregone, that is by (in this case) $(a/P - Y/P) = c(1 - Y/a)$, after substituting the value of $P = a/c$. The social value of this cost of the increased disutilities of effort, in terms of savings will be $\lambda c(1 - Y/a)/s$, and hence the *SWR* in the Harris-Todaro-Harberger-type migration model will be:
$$SWR = c - c(1 - Y/a)/s + \lambda c(1 - Y/a)/s$$
$$= c - c(1 - Y/a)(1 - \lambda)/s$$
Once again if we make the Harris-Todaro assumption that $Y = a$, then the *SWR* $= c$, the industrial wage, irrespective of the values of λ and s. While if $\lambda = 1$ (which is Harberger's assumption), then irrespective of the value of s and any divergence between Y and a, the industrial wage c, is again the *SWR*.
In our more realistic migration model however, the supply price of each migrant is $(a + d + u) = L$. The number of migrants with each industrial job created are $N = 1/P = (c - w)/(L - w)$. The net change in disutilities socially valued is then $\lambda (LN - YN)/s = \lambda [(L - Y)(c - w)/(L - w)]/s$, and the *SWR* is:
$$SWR = c - [c - (Y + \lambda (L - Y))(c - w)/(L - w)]/s$$
If $\lambda = 0$, the above expression reduces to (19) above, while if $\lambda = 1$ the *SWR* $= c - [c - L(c - w)/(L - w)]/s$, and once again none of the simpler derivations of the *SWR* of the Harris-Todaro and Harberger types will hold.

[18]As most writers have not included rural-urban migration in their models for determining the *SWR*, this aspect is neglected in this section. The previous section has already dealt with the *SWR's* derived or derivable from the Harris-Todaro-Harberger-type models and a model developed in Lal [18].

on capital above. A number of reasons have been advanced by the present author, why it may also be desirable to assume that $\lambda = 0$, for developing countries.[19] However, the values assigned to these parameters must be in the nature of value judgments, and hence the possibility of conflicting advice on the different procedures. However, as this section has tried to show, if the same assumptions and value judgments are made, the alternative procedures will give identical answers, based upon the general expression for the SWR provided by (21) above.

---

[19]See Lal [18].

III. Income Distribution and Employment

Traditionally questions of equity have been separated from those of efficiency in project analysis. This corresponds to the concern of most welfare economists with Pareto improvements which assume a given income distribution, and their inability to provide any value-free criteria for welfare improvements which involve distributional considerations. Strict adherents of a value-free welfare economics therefore are loth to include the questions of equity into the supposedly value-free efficiency criteria that can be derived from welfare economics, on the grounds that the economist qua economist has no special expertise in dealing with equity questions which involve value-judgments, and hence he should stick to his last. Thus Harberger [13] has recently stated three basic postulates of applied welfare economics, the third of which says: "when evaluating the net benefits or costs of a given action (project, program, or policy), the costs and benefits or costs accruing to each member of the relevant group (e.g., a nation) should normally be added without regard to the individual(s) to whom they accrue."[1]

---

[1]Samuelson's comment, at an earlier occasion when Harberger argued a similar case, is worth quoting:
"I am reminded of the case where a jury must determine which of two stones is heavier. The first stone can allegedly be weighed to a high degree of numerical accuracy (dollar efficiency measures). The second cannot in principle be so weighed (value-judgment decisions). What is the point in measuring the first stone if in the end we must put that exact weight in the balance with the second—particularly if, as is the true case, the two stones have no independent existence and weights? Harberger's valid defense would be to admit he is really trying to make estimates of possibility-frontier shifts. To answer, as he did to Vickrey, that since economists are no good at weighing the second stone they should concentrate on weighing the first is to fall prey to the pathetic fallacy that the universe was created to keep economists busy at something or other." P. Samuelson, "Comment on 'Principles of Efficiency'." *American Economic Review* [*Papers and Proceedings*] LIV (1964): 93-96. Harberger's paper in this symposium is "The Measurement of Waste" [LIV: 58-76] and the basic position argued therein is the same as in his [13].

In contrast with this view, there is a growing feeling among practitioners in the development field that some account needs to be taken of the distributional impact of projects. The argument is that it is only *if* (on the lines of traditional welfare economics) the government can legislate the optimum income distribution independently of project choice, that the problems of equity and efficiency can be separated. The efficiency effects of projects would then be the only concern of the project evaluator, as they would determine whether or not the project represented a Paretian improvement; the income distribution effects of the project being neutralized by appropriate tax-subsidy measures. However, even in this case, if the administrative costs of fiscal redistribution are *not* negligible, it may be necessary to take account of the distributional effects of projects, as project selection will provide an alternative redistribution mechanism (with possibly lower adminstrative costs) than that provided by the fiscal mechanism. Moreover, if there are constraints on fiscal policy and the above measures to attain the optimal income distribution are infeasible, project choice itself becomes an instrument of government policy in changing the income distribution in the desired manner. Income distribution considerations, therefore, may need to be taken into account for second best reasons, in project analysis.

The first problem in taking account of distributional effects is the assessment of the incidence of the costs and benefits of the project. In practice for some projects, it may be extremely difficult to attribute the distribution of project costs and benefits to different groups. If this attribution problem can be overcome, the next question is whether these distributional effects should be taken account of in a systematic manner in project analysis, by differentially weighting the project benefits and costs in terms of the individuals who receive or incur the costs and benefits. Or should the distributional effects merely be described (and if so, how), along with the calculation of the efficiency rates of return; leaving the weighting of the distributional effects, and any trade-off there may be between them and the efficiency rates to return to the policy maker? The disadvantages of following the latter course are that it is likely that distributional effects will be taken into account in an ad hoc manner, the implicit weights varying inconsistently from project to project.

Determining Distributional Weights

If then distributional effects are to be taken into account, how should this be done? Note firstly that there are at least two dimensions to the distributional effects of projects. The first consists of the intertemporal distribution of benefits, which will be determined by the division of the project's incomes between current consumption and savings. This was the aspect we have already discussed in our discussions of distortions in the capital market in the last section. As long as the government feels that the present level of savings is not optimal (the growth rate of the economy is not optimal) and wants to use project choice to raise the level of savings, then it is implicitly saying that present consumption is less socially valuable than future consumption (savings). The way in which this aspect can be taken into account in project analysis has already been discussed in the section on capital, and we will not discuss it further, except for noting one important feature of the necessary adjustment.

The value of s, that is the premium on current savings over current consumption, which we had discussed, depends upon the solution of a Ramsey-type formulation of intertemporal optimality, which requires the specification of an intertemporal social welfare function. Given such a welfare function which determines the distributional weights to be attached to consumption accruing to different generations (the values of d_t),[2] the same welfare function can be used to derive distributional weights to be attached to consumption accruals amongst contemporaries within a generation. The simplest way to see how these weights can be determined, is to ask the question, which income group's marginal consumption gains are socially valuable at par. Let the group whose per capita income is Y^*, be such a group. Then, *ex hypothesi,* the distributional weight attached to their income changes must be unity. Furthermore, assuming that the social weight attaching to marginal changes in the consumption of higher income groups declines in a regular fashion, the set of distributional weights to be attached to different income groups can be depicted by Figure 2.

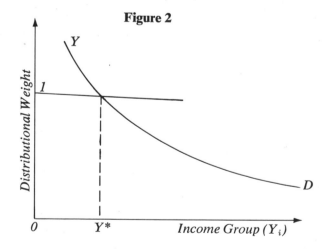

Figure 2

---

[2]d_t is the social rate of discount (LM consumption rate of interest) in period t, as explained above in Chapter II's section on *Capital.*

Thus to determine the distributional weights it is only necessary to fix the base level Y^*, and the slope of the line YD. If we assume as before that the elasticity of social marginal utility in consumption is a constant e, (see p. 28f), then the distributional weight (d_i) for any marginal change in income of income group Y_i, will be given by

$$d_i = (Y^*/Y_i)^e$$

This will determine the intratemporal distribution weights, which can be used to convert current consumption changes accruing to different contemporaries, into its social aggregate consumption equivalent. Finally, the *intertemporal* distribution of income can be accounted for by making use of s, the premium on current savings. That is the change in consumption ΔC_i of income group Y_i, is first converted into its social aggregate consumption equivalent $d_i \Delta C_i$, and then this is revalued in terms of savings (assuming that is the numeraire) as $d_i \Delta C_i/s$.[3] Hence the inter-*cum*-intratemporal distributional weight (w) for income class Y_i, will be $w_i = d_i/s = (Y^*/Y_i)^e/s$. Thus distributional weights which reflect both the intertemporal and intratemporal distributional considerations can be derived. However, these weights necessarily depend upon explicit value judgments—in the above case on the base income level Y^* and the value of the elasticity of marginal utility of a constant elasticity utility function which is used to value consumption increases both intertemporally and intratemporally. Various alternative values of this value parameter can be tried out. The policymaker can then make his choice by examining the quantitative implications of different values of the parameter.

For many, however, such a procedure will appear to be akin to "mathematical politics." An alternative would be to include only the intertemporal distributional (growth) aspects in the rate of return, and in addition present a meaningful statistic which would provide the policymaker with the important intratemporal distributional features of the project, which he could then implicitly weight against the efficiency *cum* growth rate of return of the project.

The Employment Problem

In deriving such a statistic it may be useful to consider another seemingly different problem which has been suggested as worthy of inclusion as an objective in project choice-employment. The employment problem in developing countries is essentially the problem of poverty—of raising the incomes of large numbers of people who are below some national poverty line. There are other aspects of the employment problem, namely the efficiency aspects which relate to the surplus of labor time which may be available for productive employment if the supply of cooperant factors of production could be

---

[3]The present author has derived such weights for India which also take account of regional income-differentials using a slightly more complicated derivation. See Lal [19].

increased. This is the aspect which will be taken into account by the output foregone component (m) in the *SWR's* we discussed in the section on distortions in the labor market. There is also the growth aspect of employment which is connected with the implications of increasing employment on the consumption-savings balance of the economy when the level of savings is nonoptimal in the economy—a subject we have discussed in the section on distortions in the capital market and which is again incorporated in the *SWR* in the social valuation of any net changes in aggregate consumption caused by paying labor a wage higher than its supply price (if private disutilities are socially valued, otherwise, above its alternative *VMP*). Note this is also the aspect concerned with the intertemporal distribution of project benefits. Over and above these there may still be an employment problem in the sense that it may be desirable to choose projects the benefits of which accrue to "poor" people as the provision of "employment" on the project may be the only feasible way of increasing their incomes.

The relevant distributional statistic from this poverty viewpoint will be the numbers of the poor who are benefited by the project. Such a statistic, labeled the poverty redressal index (*PRI*), has been developed by the present author (see Lal [20]). It gives the number of people below the poverty line, per unit of annual domestic resource cost, whose annual incomes are raised in perpetuity by the project. The *PRI* requires only minimal value judgments, and is relatively easy to compute. It could be used as a crude measure of the most important distributional effects of projects—the numbers of the poor whose incomes have been raised by the project per Rs expended.

If more sophisticated distributional considerations are required to be incorporated into project choice, then specification of the social welfare function and the derivation of differential weights is unavoidable.

In conclusion, it should be noted that both *LM* and UNIDO are in agreement that differential income distribution weights should be used in project analysis, and that the "employment problem" in developing countries is chiefly a problem of income distribution and poverty.

IV. Debt Servicing and Balance of Payments Problems

One of the serious practical problems facing many developing countries is the servicing of their past debts, and many people are puzzled by the seeming neglect of the debt servicing problem in investment appraisal criteria. We shall show that this is not the case and that both the basic evaluation procedures, the *LM* and the UNIDO *SER* methods, implicitly take account of it.

First note that the debt servicing problem is just the old "transfer problem"[1] and the requirements for affecting a requisite transfer are identical to the requirements for the correction of an equivalent trade imbalance. Hence the welfare costs of effecting a given transfer (which would have to be taken into account in project analysis) are identical to the welfare costs of correcting an equivalent balance of payments deficit.

Now consider the *LM* procedures. They revalue all inputs and outputs (current and future) in terms of foreign exchange. Debt service charges (and capital inflows) are included as foreign exchange costs or benefits in the year they are incurred. This assumes that the foreign loan is tied to the project. If the loan is not tied to the project, the country has first to decide whether that loan is worth accepting given the *ARI,* and various other national parameters. In this calculation the net social benefits to the country from the loan taking account of inflows and outflows on the foreign capital account, and of the likely future balance of payments and savings positions are obtained on the assumption that the loan will be invested to earn at least as much as the *ARI.* If in general the loan is acceptable, at the second stage a particular project will be evaluated conventionally and accepted as long as it has a positive *NPV* at the *ARI.* Thus, the debt servicing problem will have been

---

[1]The "transfer problem" concerned the real costs of efficient foreign transfers (specifically reparations from Germany in the interwar debates).

taken into account at the first stage.[2] The foreign exchange benefits which form the net social benefit of the project in any year are therefore net of the debt service charges, and hence debt servicing is directly included in the time stream of the costs of the project.

On the *SER* method, again the debt service charges are included in the costs of the project. But as these procedures use domestic currency as the numeraire, the foreign currency value of the debt service costs has to be converted into domestic social costs at the *SER* in that year. The net social benefits in the time stream of benefits and costs of the project will therefore be net of the debt servicing charges.

In both procedures, if the social rate of return, taking account of these debt service charges, is higher than the relevant discount rate, the project is acceptable and, *ex hypothesi* cannot create a debt servicing problem for the country. Hence the rates of return on both the *LM* and *SER* methods are full social rates of return which already include the debt servicing costs created by the project. No further adjustment therefore needs to be made for debt servicing on these procedures.

It may be felt however that in the future the country may be faced by a *general* debt servicing problem, which is equivalent to saying that in the future a general balance of payments problem is expected. How will the alternative procedures deal with this? The answer has already been given, in part, in our discussion of trade distortions, when we discussed how shadow prices would change on the alternative procedures with trade liberalization accompanied by a flexible exchange rate and fixed money prices of domestic (nontraded) goods. We will however for completeness spell it out in detail, this time in terms of textbook balance of payments theory.

It is well known that a balance of payments deficit (B) is exactly equal to the excess of domestic expenditure (E) over domestic output (income) (Y). That is, $B = Y - E$. To cure this deficit it is necessary in general to use two instruments: one to switch the pattern of expenditure to domestic goods, the second to reduce the level of domestic expenditure. Assume that the government always maintains internal balance by appropriate expenditure reducing/increasing policies. In addition, to cure the balance of payments deficit. the pattern of expenditure will have to be switched, by some means, away from traded to nontraded (domestic) goods. If the price of domestic (nontraded) goods is inflexible, the only way for this expenditure switching to take place is via an exchange rate change. As a result, the prices of traded goods, *in domestic currency,* will be higher in the postdevaluation, as compared with

[2]For a discussion of this type of calculation and the derivation of the relevant rules, see D. Lal, "When is Foreign Borrowing Desirable?" *Bulletin of Oxford University Institute of Economics and Statistics* 33 (1971): 197-206.

the predevaluation situation, and will also be higher relative to the price of nontraded goods, the prices of which have been assumed to remain constant. Working in *domestic currency,* therefore, the prices of traded goods will have to be multiplied by the anticipated postdevaluation exchange rate, to give the higher domestic currency equivalents in the postdevaluation situation, and hence the higher relative price of traded to nontraded goods which is necessary to cure the incipient balance of payments deficit caused by the transfer problem. Equivalently we could have obtained the correct relative prices of traded to nontraded goods by working in *foreign currency* and following the *LM* procedures. On the *LM* procedures as we have seen, the foreign currency costs of the *MSC* of producing the nontraded goods will be the shadow price of these goods. With an anticipated devaluation the *foreign* currency value of the *MSC* of producing the nontraded goods will fall. With the *domestic* money price of nontraded goods assumed constant, the fall in their foreign currency shadow price is equivalent to an *implicit* deflation of the domestic money price by the postdevaluation exchange rate (which is the postdevaluation *SER* on the alternative method).

To see how the foreign currency value of the *MSC* of production of nontraded goods falls with an anticipated devaluation, we have to consider what happens to the *LM SWR* with a devaluation. For the other costs of production are, *ex hypothesi,* tradeables (as the costs of production are broken down, until they comprise tradeables and labor on the *LM* method), whose *foreign currency value is* fixed, and will not alter with an exchange rate alteration. The only component of the costs of producing nontradeables, in foreign currency, which can change is the foreign exchange value of the *SWR.*[3]

From our discussion of labor above we have the *LM SWR* as $SWR = c - (c - m)/s$ where c is now the *foreign currency value* of the money wage, w, labor receives. The supply of labor is moreover assumed to be elastic at this constant money wage, w. The alternative output foregone by using labor is also constant; its value *in foreign currency* being m. As before, s is the premium on savings vis-à-vis current consumption. Thus all the components of the *SWR* are given in foreign currency, and hence the foreign currency value (shadow price) of the nontraded good is determined. With an anticipated devaluation, *ceteris paribus,* the foreign exchange value of the traded good inputs, and the m component in the *SWR* used to determine the costs of production of the nontraded good (in foreign currency) will not change. However, *given our assumption of a constant money wage w, its foreign currency value c will fall.* Hence from the *SWR* formula it can be seen that for this reason the *SWR* will fall (in foreign currency), and thus the nontraded good price (in terms of foreign currency) will fall. This is the *LM* analogue

---

[3]Assuming for simplicity, no skilled and/or self-employed labor.

to the *SER* procedures for taking account of the expenditure switching aspect of the balance of payments adjustment process.

There is in addition, however, another countervailing influence on the *SWR*. As noted above, in addition to the exchange rate change (for switching expenditure) there will also have to be a reduction in domestic expenditure to correct the incipient balance of payments deficit. If it is assumed that aggregate domestic consumption cannot be cut (a simplifying assumption) the impact of the expenditure reduction must fall on domestic investment. But this must imply that the social return to investment, the *LM* accounting rate of interest (*ARI*), *will rise*. As aggregate consumption has not been affected, the social rate of time preference (the *LM* consumption rate of interest, *CRI*) remains constant. This implies that the divergence between the *ARI* and *CRI* (which determines the premium on current savings *s*) increases, and hence *s* rises.[4] This increase in *s, ceteris paribus,* will tend to *raise the SWR*.[5] The net effect on the *SWR* will thus be the result of the twin policies needed to correct an incipient trade imbalance: an exchange rate change (switch in the pattern of expenditure) which changes the value of *c* (measured in foreign currency) and a change in the level of expenditure, which changes the level of *s* by raising the *ARI*.

Finally, the rise in the *ARI* will mean that the cutoff *IRR* for accepting a project will rise, and hence the lower level of investment which is needed to get the expenditure reduction will be achieved. But note that the cut in investment should be across the board, for with the shadow prices in the post-devaluation situation being used to evaluate projects, the relative shadow prices for all the goods are correct, and hence *all* investment projects which have a lower social rate of return than the higher *ARI* should be cut back.

---

[4]This can be clearly seen from equation (7) above, where p_t is the *ARI* and d_t is the *CRI*.

[5]Strictly speaking our simplifying assumption that aggregate domestic consumption cannot be cut is inconsistent with our earlier assumption that the money wage is fixed, and hence the real wage falls with a devaluation. The fall in the real wage will obviously imply some fall in private consumption. This will tend to raise the *LM* consumption rate of interest (*CRI*), and for a given *ARI* will tend to reduce the divergence between the *ARI* and *CRI* (note that normally the *CRI* < *ARI*), and hence *reduce s*. The effect of the cut in investment and government expenditure, which will concomitantly be required to reduce total domestic absorption to improve the balance of payments, will be (as stated in the text), to raise the *ARI,* and hence for any given *CRI* to increase the divergence between the *CRI* and *ARI* and hence *raise s*. The net effects of expenditure reduction on *s* and hence on the *SWR* will then depend upon the opposing effects of cuts in private consumption and investment and government expenditure on *s*. On balance, however, the value of *s* is likely to *rise* with expenditure reduction necessary to improve the balance of payments, as the *proportionate* cuts in domestic investment and government expenditure will generally be more severe than those in private consumption. A rise in *s,* naturally, will lead to a *rise in the SWR,* as derived in the text.

Note that on the *SER* procedures, too, the level of domestic expenditure has to be cut back, and given the same assumption about the inflexibility of consumption expenditure, the expenditure reduction must fall on investment, thereby raising the social return to investment, and raising the discount rate with which the *IRR* of projects should be compared.

Thus both the *LM* and *SER* methods take account of an incipient balance of payments (transfer) problem in equivalent ways, by first altering the relative price of traded to nontraded goods, and second by reducing domestic expenditure by raising the cut-off *IRR* for accepting projects.

There are therefore no special adjustments necessary on either method to take account of the debt servicing problems associated with specific projects, or with any general debt servicing (balance of payments) problem which may be foreseen in the future.

V. Second-Best Problems and Differential Taxation

In our discussion so far we have dealt with specific distortions in the domestic price system, and the adjustments these call for, in a piecemeal manner. It being implicitly assumed that apart from the particular divergences between MSV's and MSC's of goods and factors we have discussed, there are no other distortions in the economy. Suppose, however, as is likely in most developing countries, that (a) there are various other *domestic* distortions which the government cannot cure because its use of certain policy instruments is constrained as being infeasible, and/or (b) that while the government has complete control over the public sector, and can legislate the "shadow" pricing rules therein, its control over the coexisting private sector is limited. What will be the correct shadow pricing rules to be adopted in such second-best situations?

The same problem can be put in a slightly different form by recognizing that one of the main sources of divergence between the MSV and MSC's of commodities/factors, is the domestic tax system. Most governments have to raise revenue for public or redistributive purposes or both by taxation. Theoretically, the only nondistortionary taxes are lump-sum taxes. In practice, however, such taxes are infeasible. Given this constraint, the feasible set of taxes will necessarily cause a divergence between the MSV and MSC's of commodities/factors. What are the correct "shadow" prices to be used? The MSV's (the marginal rates of substitution or the demand prices), the MSC's (the marginal rates of transformation or the supply prices) or a weighted average of the two? It has been shown by Diamond and Mirrlees [6] that, assuming that administrative costs are negligible, but all commodities can be taxed, the correct shadow prices to be used are *producer's prices* (that is, the MSC's) of the relevant goods/factors. The quasi-optimal taxes for raising government revenue being differential taxes on final consumer goods. The argument can be seen heuristically in terms of a simple geometric model due to Diamond-Mirrlees. We assume an economy with a single consumer, who supplies labor to the government which is used solely to produce a single consumer good X, which is sold to the consumer in payment for his labor at an "equilibrium" relative price of labor to consumer good X. The government needs to appropriate a fixed amount of the consumer's labor for its own purposes, but it cannot do so by levying a lump-sum tax on him. It can only raise the required resources by effecting the relative price of good X to labor by taxing the commodity X. What is the optimum production and tax configuration for this economy?

Figure 3 shows the production possibility set describing the feasible output of good X which the government can provide the consumer in return for his labor (PP). The distance OP represents the amount of the consumer's labor resources the government wants to appropriate, and hence the PP curve will start from P and not the origin. The curve moreover has been drawn assuming diminishing returns to scale. (The argument applies equally to constant returns to scale as can be easily checked by drawing PP as a straight line.) OC represents the locus of the points of tangency of the consumers indifference curves (between labor effort and consumption of X such as ll) with the various possible relative prices of labor and X the consumer can face. It is thus the consumer's offer curve; and represents points of consumer's "equilibrium."

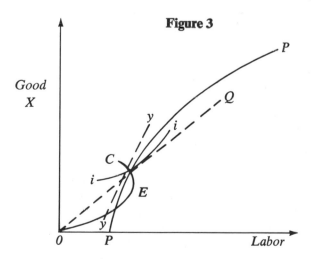

Figure 3

The government now has to chose a production point which is technologically feasible, which ensures consumer's equilibrium, and also maximizes his welfare, subject to the restriction that the government must appropriate OP of his labor, but can only do so by commodity taxation (choosing the relative price of labor to good X). It must necessarily therefore choose point E. But E is on the production frontier and hence a *productive efficient* point. To sustain the production/consumption configuration at E, the consumer price of X to labor must be set at that given by the slope of the line OEQ, while the producer price must be set equal to the marginal rate of transformation in production at E, namely that given the slope of the line yy. The difference between the producer and consumer prices gives the quasi-optimal tax on commodity X (taking the wage rate of labor as the numeraire). Thus even though lump sum taxation is infeasible, production efficiency is desirable. The result carries over to a many-commodity, many-consumer economy where all commodities except one are taxable.

However it may not be feasible for governments to levy these quasi-optimal commodity taxes. Various alternative restrictions on the government's fiscal powers may then be considered relevant. Stiglitz and Dasgupta [30] have considered models with a wide variety of restrictions on the government's fiscal powers. One obvious limiting case is one where it is assumed that all taxes are given and assumed to remain fixed. The given taxes (including tariffs) need not be optimal, and hence this case is of fairly wide relevance. For this case Dasgupta and Stiglitz [4] show that (assuming away the problems of other distortions apart from those introduced by the given fiscal system), *if there are no fixed quotas,* the shadow prices to be used for project evaluation in the public sector (and for private sector projects subject to government "control") for tradeable goods are their "border" prices, while for those for nontradeables are their marginal foreign exchange costs that is the value of the foreign exchange that would be earned if one less unit of the given nontradeables were produced and the resources diverted to the production of tradeables. While *if there are quotas,* then except for the goods subject to the quotas, for all other goods the same rules as given above apply; while for the goods subject to the fixed quota their "shadow prices" will be higher than "international prices." Hence as they conclude there is a general presumption for using "international" prices in project evaluation.

These results carry over to the cases where there is an uncontrolled private sector with constant returns to scale, or in which private producers act, or are made to act (say, through profits taxes) as perfect competitors. If the private sector requires government licensing for its investments, then it can just be regarded as part of the public sector. It is only in cases where the government cannot directly or indirectly control the private sector, and hence the prices which private producers pay or receive can affect aggregate social welfare that departures from the above shadow pricing rules will be desirable. But in such cases there are no clear cut alternative rules which can be given. Thus in general there is a presumption that the shadow pricing rules advocated by *LM* (and the equivalent *UHS* procedures) will in a wide variety of realistic second best situations lead to social welfare improvements.

References

[1] E. Bacha and L. Taylor, "Foreign Exchange Shadow Prices: A Criti-
     cal Review of Current Theories." *Quarterly Journal of Economics*
     LXXXV (1971): 197-224.
[2] M. Bruno, "The Optimal Selection of Export Promoting and Import
     Substituting Projects" in *Planning the External Sector: Techniques,
     Problems, and Policies.* New York: United Nations, 1967.
[3] J. Byer, *An Economic Framework for Project Analysis in India: Some
     Preliminary Estimates.* New Delhi: Ford Foundation, 1972.
[4] P. Dasgupta and J. E. Stiglitz, "Benefit-Cost Analysis and Trade
     Policies." Cowles Foundation Discussion Paper no. 340 [also
     forthcoming in the *Journal of Political Economy*].
[5] P. Dasgupta, "The Shadow Price of Foreign Exchange—An Exercise
     on the UNIDO Guidelines for Project Evaluation." UNIDO, ID/
     WG. 150/4. New York: United Nations, 1973.
[6] P. A. Diamond and J. A. Mirrlees, "Optimal Taxation and Public
     Production." *American Economic Review* LXI (1971): 8-27,
     261-78.
[7] A. K. Dixit, "Short-Run Equilibrium and Shadow Prices in the Dual
     Economy." *Oxford Economic Papers* 23 (1971): 384-400.
[8] R. Dorfman, P. A. Samuelson, and R. M. Solow, *Linear Program-
     ming and Economic Analysis.* New York: McGraw Hill (Rand
     Series), 1958.
[9] M. H. Dobb, *An Essay on Economic Growth and Planning.* London:
     Routledge & Paul, 1960.

[10] W. Galenson and H. Leibenstein, "Investment Criteria, Productivity and Economic Development." *Quarterly Journal of Economics* LXIX (1955): 343-70.

[11] A. C. Harberger, "Survey of Literature on Cost-Benefit Analysis for Industrial Project Evaluation" in *Evaluation of Industrial Projects.* New York: United Nations (UNIDO), 1968.

[12] A. C. Harberger, "The Social Opportunity Cost of Labour." *International Labour Review* 103 (1971): 559-79.

[13] A. C. Harberger, "Three Basic Postulates of Applied Welfare Economics." *Journal of Economic Literature* IX (1971): 785-97.

[14] J. R. Harris and M. P. Todaro, "Migration, Unemployment and Development: A Two-Sector Analysis." *American Economic Review* LX (1970): 126-42.

[15] A. E. Kahn, "Investment Criteria in Development Programs." *Quarterly Journal of Economics* LXV (1951): 38-61.

[16] A. O. Kruger, "Some Economic Costs of Exchange Control: The Turkish Case." *Journal of Political Economy* LXXIV (1966): 466-80.

[17] D. Lal, "Adjustment for Trade Distortions in Project Analysis." IBRD Economic Staff Working Paper no. 128, mimeographed. Washington, D.C., 1972 [also forthcoming in the *Journal of Development Studies*].

[18] D. Lal, "Disutility of Effort, Migration and the Shadow Wage Rate." *Oxford Economic Papers* 25 (1973): 112-26.

[19] D. Lal, "On Estimating Income—Distribution Weights for Project Analysis." IBRD Economic Staff Working Paper no. 130, mimeographed. Washington, D.C., 1972.

[20] D. Lal, "Employment, Income Distribution and a Poverty Redressal Index." IBRD Economic Staff Working Paper no. 129, mimeographed. Washington, D.C., 1972 [also in *World Development* I (February 1973)].

[21] D. Lal, *Wells and Welfare.* Paris: Organization for Economic Cooperation and Development, 1972.

[22] D. Lal, "On Estimating Certain Intertemporal Parameters for Project Analysis." IBRD mimeograph. Washington, D.C., 1973.

[23] W. A. Lewis, "Economic Development with Unlimited Supplies of Labour." *Manchester School of Economics and Social Sciences* 22 (1954): 139-91.

[24] I. M. D. Little and J. A. Mirrlees, *Manual of Industrial Project Analysis in Developing Countries, Volume II: Social Cost-Benefit Analysis.* Paris: Organization for Economic Cooperation and Development, 1968.

[25] I. M. D. Little and J. A. Mirrlees, "A Reply to Some Criticisms of the OECD Manual." *Bulletin of Oxford University Institute of Economics and Statistics* [since volume 35 (1973), the *Oxford Bulletin of Economics and Statistics*] 34 (1972): 153-68.

[26] S. A. Marglin, *Public Investment Criteria.* Cambridge, Mass.: MIT Press, 1967.

[27] D. M. Schydlowsky, "On the Choice of a Shadow Price for Foreign Exchange." Economic Development Report no. 108. Cambridge, Mass.: Development Advisory Service, Center for International Affairs, Harvard University, 1968.

[28] A. K. Sen, "Peasants and Dualism With and Without Surplus Labor." *Journal of Political Economy* LXXIV (1966): 425-50.

[29] A. K. Sen, *Choice of Techniques, An Aspect of the Theory of Planned Economic Development.* 3rd ed. Oxford: B. Blackwell, 1968.

[30] J. E. Stiglitz and P. Dasgupta, "Differential Taxation, Public Goods and Economic Efficiency." *Review of Economic Studies* XXXVIII (1971): 151-74.

[31] M. P. Todaro, "A Model of Labor Migration and Urban Unemployment in Less Developed Countries." *American Economic Review* LIX (1969): 138-48.

[32] United Nations Industrial Development Organization [P. Dasgupta, A. Sen, and S. Marglin], *Guidelines for Project Evaluation.* New York: United Nations, 1972.

Library of Congress Cataloging in Publication Data

Lal, Deepak.
  Methods of project analysis: a review

  (World Bank staff occasional papers, no. 16)
  Bibliography: p.
  1. Cost effectiveness. 2. Underdeveloped areas—
Prices. I. Title. II. Series
HD 47.5.L25   338.1/3   73-20916
ISBN 0-8018-1615-7